Inhabiting Eden

Inhabiting Eden

Christians, the Bible, and the Ecological Crisis

Patricia K. Tull

WESTMINSTER
JOHN KNOX PRESS
LOUISVILLE · KENTUCKY

© 2013 Patricia K. Tull

First edition
Published by Westminster John Knox Press
Louisville, Kentucky

14 15 16 17 18 19 20 21 22—10 9 8 7 6 5 4 3 2

Book design by Sharon Adams
Cover design by Dilu Nicholas
Cover illustration: Lonely tree in the desert at sunset © Andrey Voskressenskiy/shutterstock.com

Library of Congress Cataloging-in-Publication Data

Tull, Patricia K.
Inhabiting Eden : Christians, the Bible, and the ecological crisis / Patricia K. Tull. — First edition.
    pages cm
Includes bibliographical references.
ISBN 978-0-664-23333-4 (alk. paper)
  1. Human ecology—Religious aspects—Christianity. 2. Bible. Genesis I–IV—Criticism, interpretation, etc. I. Title.
BT695.5.T85 2013
261.8'8—dc23

2013020785

Most Westminster John Knox Press books are available at special quantity discounts when purchased in bulk by corporations, organizations, and special-interest groups. For more information, please e-mail SpecialSales@wjkbooks.com.

Contents

Acknowledgments

Several colleagues and friends commented on portions of this book as it was being written, including Andrew Bartlett, Tim Darst, Amanda Shepherd, Wendy Bronson, Susan Smith, Lorna Kuyk, Melissa Rue, Brad Wigger, Jennifer Mills-Knutsen, Peter Smith, Cory Lockhart, and especially Anne Vouga, who patiently read it all. Several members of First Presbyterian Church of Jeffersonville, Indiana, met together to read and offer constructive critique of each chapter, and I thank them for their insights: Doyle Criswell, Carissa Herold, Nancy and Pat Ohlmann, Ray and Yvonne Knight, Virgil Hertling, and Don Summerfield. I also thank several Louisville, Kentucky groups for invitations to preach and teach: Central Presbyterian, Crescent Hill Presbyterian, Bardstown Road Presbyterian, Buechel Park Baptist, Highland Baptist, Anchorage Presbyterian, and Louisville Presbyterian Theological Seminary.

Thanks go also to Gary Eller, president of the Omaha Presbyterian Seminary Foundation, who invited me to present early chapters in the summer school for pastors in Hastings, Nebraska, in July 2011, and to members of that class for conversations over the pastoral dimensions of farming. Thanks also to Nuha Khoury and Andreas Kuntz, who invited me to give a public lecture at Dar al-Kalima University in Bethlehem in February 2012, and to Palestinians who conversed with me about ecological issues in their region; to Fletcher Harper and Jerry Cappel of GreenFaith for the invitation to lead workshops in Charlotte, North Carolina, in October 2012; to the Ecological Hermeneutics section of the Society of Biblical Literature for the opportunity to present a portion of this work in progress; and to Ben McDonald Coltvet of workingpreacher.org, who invited me to write a monthly lectionary column based on this work.

Various local and national organizations have created a web of friends whose understandings have enriched my own, including the Climate Reality Project, the Community Farm Alliance, the Passionist Earth and Spirit Center, Healthy Farms Local Foods, Purdue University's Agricultural Extension program, Interfaith Power and Light, Ghost Ranch, and Louisville's Festival of Faiths. Thanks especially to Father Joe Mitchell and Father Nelson Alphonse, and to Nelson's parents Carolyn and Alphonse, who showed me the landscape and some of the farming practices of South India, and to Bhuwon and Rajya Sthapit, who taught me about land and sustainable seed in the hills of Nepal. Conversations with many allies and friends have enriched my thinking, including Rebecca Barnes, Larry Rasmussen, Bill Brown, Scott Russell Sanders, Keith Mountain, Margaret Carreiro, Sarah Lynn Cunningham, Father John Rausch, and Sister Robbie Pentecost, as well as local farmers David and Gail Crum, David and Esther Miller, and Mary Graf. I've appreciated opportunities to hear directly from leaders such as Wendell Berry, Wes Jackson, Sally Bingham, Eric Schlosser, Alice Waters, and Al Gore.

I am grateful to editors at Westminster John Knox Press, especially Jon Berquist, who invited me to write this book, and Alicia Samuels, with whom I finished it. I am grateful for Alicia's guidance and for many enjoyable conversations over our respective gardening projects. Thanks also go to Julie Tonini, Erika Lundbom, and Emily Kiefer for their work in producing and distributing the book.

Most and best, I thank my dear spouse Don for many years of conversation, conservation projects and classes together, arboretums explored, and trees planted. I am grateful to our six offspring and the increasing number of young adults who, through them, have joined our family, and who have tolerated and even embraced our way of life. This book is dedicated to the grandchildren who as yet live only in our children's imaginations, and our own.

Do not remember the former things,
or consider the things of old.
I am about to do a new thing;
now it springs forth, do you not perceive it?
—Isaiah 43:18–19

We are discovering that the human heart is not changed by facts alone but by engaging visions and empowering values. Humans need to see the large picture and feel they can act to make a difference.
—Mary Evelyn Tucker and John Grim, "Daring to Dream: Religion and the Future of the Earth," *Yale University Reflections Magazine*

Chapter 1

The Problem of Change, Then and Now

The Challenge

One January I was traveling in South India with my daughter Claire, who lives in Nepal. When our host in Coimbatore took us to the train station to return to Bangalore, he boarded with us, settling us across the aisle from a nun in full habit, explaining to her in Tamil who we were, where we were going, and for all we knew, how ignorant we were about Indian transit. She nodded in our direction. She was wearing the white and blue habit of Mother Teresa's Missionaries of Charity, and I was entranced. All my romanticism about Mother Teresa, about nuns, and about travel in India drowned out apprehensions about finding our way.

We set out among the mountains. Throughout South India's flatlands, everywhere we had traveled, along every road, we had passed masses of people working, walking, driving, biking, sitting, eating, sweeping, bathing, cooking, laughing—as if all humanity had congregated on the tip of South Asia to sink it. But there was no road beside this track, and for the first time in three weeks we saw open countryside, mountains almost close enough to touch. I smiled at my daughter and then at the sister, who was eating her lunch, a box of chicken. We ate a couple of bananas and I looked for a waste bin and, finding none, wondered if it was proper to throw the peels from the train. The sister finished her chicken,

1

stood up, leaned over the two people sitting between her and the open window, and tossed box, drinking cup, napkins, fork, bones, the whole litter of a fast food meal, into the mountain, and then sat down and took out a prayer book.

It's tempting to shrug and say, that's a different culture. But on the Ohio River near our house, hundreds of thousands congregate for the annual fireworks display that wakes up all creation, Thunder over Louisville. The trash that strews roads and sidewalks from the river to downtown the next morning puts American manners badly on display. This is something more: a mentality that the earth is our waste bin.

Once I was talking to a colleague, a left-leaning scholar, in her office. She commended me for some environmental deed or another as she threw an empty, recyclable Coke bottle into her waste basket.

I tell these stories not because they are so egregious but because they are so common. If being religious, or being in public, or even being verbally committed to ecological causes cannot help us reexamine small actions, what will change us in the large ones? I myself am just as guilty: if the nun trashed the mountainside, I had trashed the stratosphere by jetting across the world, even if it was to see my daughter. Although ecological awareness has often inspired me to stay put, it has not led me to cease flying altogether. And perhaps this is part of the issue—we are social beings, and while some may be more committed than others to improving ecological behavior, we are limited both by personal habits and by what society as a whole makes possible.

In his book *The Creation*, written as a letter to Christian preachers, Harvard biologist E. O. Wilson calls religion and science "the two most powerful forces in the world today." He comments:

> If religion and science could be united on the common ground
> of biological conservation, the problem would soon be solved.
> If there is any moral precept shared by people of all beliefs, it is
> that we owe ourselves and future generations a beautiful, rich,
> and healthful environment.[1]

We may search for technological answers to the multiple ecological problems we face, but the questions are really human ones: What do we value? How do our lives and values line up? Do we see ourselves as part of the magnificent web of life, or do we, like Esau, trade our birthright for a momentary mess of stew?

Wilson argues that science can provide information about the biosphere, "the totality of all life, creator of all air, cleanser of all water, manager of all soil, but itself a fragile membrane that barely clings to the face of the planet."[2] Religious leaders, he said, help shape awareness of and gratitude for this complex and tender sphere. There can be no change in action without changes in perception of who we are and to whom and what we owe allegiance.

This book is written as a resource for people who look to the Bible for guidance in contemporary life. Scripture doesn't by any means tell us all that we might like to understand. But if we remove some modern blinders we will find it says a great deal more than we think about our ties with the rest of creation, ties we must now reclaim, ties that will not only lead us into restoring our surroundings, but into joys that consumer culture cannot offer.

Scripture tells us that our original forebears lost the garden of Eden before they realized what they had. Not ever having been there myself, I have trouble picturing a world more exquisite than our own. It's not just the snowcapped peak of Fishtale Mountain behind my daughter's house in Pokhara, nor the vast red hues of the Grand Canyon, nor the Smoky Mountains and Shenandoah Valley. It's the mockingbird practicing its repertoire in the burning bush; it's the maple tree in the backyard, changing with the seasons from greens to oranges to intricate, rugged browns. Each locale has its bits of Eden, habitats to inherit, enjoy, tend, and bequeath to our descendants.

We are approaching a turning point in history, one that will tell us whether we truly are the Homo sapiens, the "wise ones," we call ourselves. It's time to dig into our spiritual heritage to find wisdom for crucial decisions that face us all.

The Problem of Precedent

We are not alone in this. Every generation faces challenges for which our upbringing has not directly prepared us—challenges economic, military, moral, religious, and social. To overcome problems our parents and grandparents did not foresee, we find ourselves forced to reexamine established assumptions. Change is hard enough for individuals. It is far more difficult to motivate a whole society to work together, particularly in a time as contentious and individualistic as our own. Until a critical mass of people are convinced of the necessity, convinced in heart and soul as well as mind, change does not take root. Such conviction is hard to find when the crisis is unprecedented. What the world has not seen before, we resist seeing now.

Christians who rely on Scripture for guidance are sometimes dismayed that the Bible does not give clear direction about contemporary issues unknown to the ancient world. We search the Bible to see whether passages overlooked in the past, when asked new questions, may offer unforeseen wisdom. This study contends that careful reading of Scripture can indeed lend insight for approaching the current ecological crisis.

This crisis is both multifaceted and urgent. Despite strides made over the past several decades, challenges continue to intensify:

- *Water:* Because of overuse and misuse, and because of increasing population, drought, and pollution, fewer and fewer of the earth's people enjoy access to clean, drinkable water. What was once seen as a basic right is being commodified as the "new gold." Many say that the next war will not be fought over oil, but water. Oceans are warming and acidifying, and seas are overfished. Nitrogen runoff from farming has created algae blooms that kill ocean plants and animals, creating large dead zones along the coasts.
- *Land use:* As the population not only expands numerically but demands more, wild lands worldwide have vanished into suburban sprawl and industrial farms. Topsoil

is disappearing. Tropical rainforests are being clearcut
for timber and for cattle grazing. Species that made their
homes in these places have become extinct, upsetting
nature's balance.

- *Trash and toxic waste*: Nonbiodegradable waste is filling
the planet. In each of the earth's oceans floats a large
patch of plastic waste. Some say that the Pacific Garbage
Patch is as large as the United States, poisoning sea creatures that try to feed from it. Industries and individuals
use the air, water, and ground as toxic garbage dumps,
sickening people and other life. Newer generations of
electronic toys have created new toxicities as computer
waste is dumped into landfills or sent to developing countries for dismantling, exposing families to toxic metals.

- *Energy*: Increasingly over the past century, most of our
energy has come from nonrenewable coal, oil, and natural gas. As these resources become less accessible, it takes
more energy and more risk to mine them. Wars are being
fought over access. As the population increases and as
more people prosper, demand and competition are rising.

- *Climate Change*: According to environmental scientists
worldwide, other problems pale next to the swiftly growing crisis of global climate change, signaled by severe
weather events such as heat waves, droughts, deluges, and
hurricanes. Immediate, broadscale energy conservation
measures and development of renewable energy can prevent destruction of life as we know it. Though scientists
agree that the problems are severe but solvable, political debates—especially in the United States—continue to
stall meaningful action.

We've Always Done It This Way

As humans we can cure these ills, but only if we accept the challenge of change. We tend toward inertia, toward thinking that
whatever we grew up with was normative, even our God-given

right. In the United States we have believed in unlimited resources and ever-increasing wealth, yesterday's luxuries becoming today's entitlements. Yet since the world began, change has never ceased. Insofar as change promises to bring more of the life to which we would like to become accustomed, we embrace it. But there is no rule that says change will always be onward and upward; in fact, history shows that changes can also worsen conditions. We need not look past Hurricane Katrina in 2005 or the economic crisis of 2008 to see this. When such shifts occur, failure to adjust expectations can exacerbate otherwise solvable problems. This is not negativity, but realism.

Yet the need for change is nothing new. The human story consists of a series of crisis points—moments when people have been moved to reexamine assumptions, to change direction, to turn from what they were doing and follow another path, even against their convenience. As we can see in Scripture as well as in recent history, farsighted change in direction stands at the beginning of our most world-shaping moments. Scripture tells such stories: of Noah, called to save his family and every animal species from a great flood that destroyed and remade the world; of Abraham and Sarah, called to move to a land they had never seen; of the pharaoh's daughter, called to adopt a baby found along the riverbank; of Esther, called to confront the Persian emperor, saving her nation; of ordinary fishermen called to travel the Mediterranean world preaching a Jewish savior.

Not all changes are individual. In fact, named individuals hardly ever act alone. Scriptures tell, for instance, of the remaking of the Hebrew people at Sinai, promising to follow the God who delivered them from slavery; and of the reformation of the Jewish nation after the Babylonian exile, rebuilding the ruined city of Jerusalem. The book of Acts records adaptations made by the first Christian communities as they negotiated changed relationships with both Jews and Gentiles. Scripture is filled with such turning points. We will examine two of these below, one reflected in the book of the prophet Isaiah, and a second from the story of Paul in Acts. But first let's consider movements in recent history.

Abolition of British Slave Trade

The 2007 movie *Amazing Grace* tells of a British politician named William Wilberforce. His transformation began in 1786 when a group of citizens urged him to help end the buying and selling of Africans as slaves. This two-hundred-year-old practice had supported the British economy for twice as long as the auto industry has for ours today.

Up to that point, Wilberforce's Christian faith had led him to uphold British society as he knew it. But as he listened and began to learn, he recognized the unthinkable suffering this practice inflicted on others. We can imagine how it might have been for Wilberforce, confronting realities he knew but had not taken to heart, and facing earnest Christians who claimed that as a politician he could and should help change British law. Wilberforce was no social liberal—in fact, he opposed workers' rights to organize unions and women's leadership in abolitionist meetings. He was a complex person with growing convictions rooted in evangelical faith, a person becoming convinced, despite societal norms, that slaveholding was immoral.

In 1791 he introduced legislation to abolish the slave trade. The bill lost 163 to 88. Others called him unpatriotic, disloyal, and insensitive to the economic needs and even the international security of Britain. Slave trade as a source of energy and wealth was as entrenched then as fossil fuel is today. Few white people could imagine Western civilization functioning without others' forced labor.

But against all odds he persisted, introducing his bill every year for the next sixteen. In the meantime, he and a growing number of others worked to change opinions by offering tours of slave ships, putting manacles on display, and publishing slaves' autobiographies. Every year they gained more converts. And finally, one day in 1807, by a vote of 283 to 16, British slave trade was ended. This step led to slavery's abolition in the British Empire in 1834. American slaves had another generation to wait for freedom, and another century still to obtain legal rights due to all. Racism lingers still, with all its frustrations, dangers, and harms, but where would we be today without the courageous faith that kept a few people pressing for change?

Women's Equal Rights

For a Quaker minister named Lucretia Mott, the call to promote societal changes began as a rude awakening. In 1840 she and her husband James traveled to England as delegates to an abolitionist convention. James was welcomed, but Lucretia and another woman, Elizabeth Cady Stanton, were forced to sit behind heavy curtains where they could hear but not participate. Having come to advocate slaves' rights, Mott found herself deprived of speech and action. So in 1848 she and Stanton organized the first women's rights convention in Seneca Falls, New York. Thirty years later, Stanton and Susan B. Anthony persuaded California Senator Aaron Sargent to introduce a U.S. constitutional amendment for women's suffrage. It was defeated. The amendment was reintroduced each year for the next forty-one until it passed in 1920, eighty years after Lucretia Mott's rude awakening and forty years after her death. Women's suffrage took twice as long as it took the Israelites to wander their wilderness. Though the Equal Rights Amendment proposed in 1923 still stands unratified nearly a century later, women nevertheless occupy almost every office of political power.

Indeed, We Have Always Done It This Way

History consists of many such unprecedented turns from prior norms, turns sometimes angrily or even violently opposed. During the rise of Nazism in Germany seventy years ago, three-fourths of all Americans opposed letting so-called "refu-Jews" emigrate to America. Christians had found numerous ways to interpret Scripture to support their anti-Jewish prejudice. But the shock of the Holocaust led Christians to repudiate ancient beliefs. They began to learn the strength found in interfaith cooperation not only with Jews but with Muslims, Hindus, Buddhists, and other religious folk around the world.

Changes have taken place in our ecological thinking as well. A generation ago we freely used aerosol sprays filled with chlorofluorocarbons (CFCs), chemicals that destroyed the ozone layer, contributing to skin cancers, cataracts, and global warming. In 1978 the United States helped lead the world in halting these pollutants. Aerosol manufacturers themselves voluntarily changed their practices. The ozone layer now shows signs of recovery, and environmentalists celebrate this turnaround as evidence that concerned individuals, businesses, and governments can together change our behavior and the planet's future.

Every day we hear public calls to change, and never so many as when, during a crisis such as Hurricanes Katrina or Sandy, we are moved by the pain and grief of others. Not every call is divinely inspired. But when we discern God's voice beckoning us to follow a fork in the road, we can walk securely, knowing that God makes the impossible possible, creating a future from which the human race can gaze back with gratitude.

See, I'm Doing Something New

Scripture itself provides models for finding guidance in unprecedented times. The exodus from Egypt, for instance, became a powerful precedent for later generations who had likewise become refugees outside their land. According to that story, miracle after miracle had confirmed God's determination not to let any power stand in the way of Israelite freedom, resulting in their dramatic flight from Egypt to safety beyond the Red Sea, and finally to self-governance.

By the time of the Judean exile to Babylon in the early sixth century, the exodus story had become the stuff of legend. Descendants of the Israelites found themselves once again living under foreign domination, having endured unprecedented destruction in their homeland, their capital city, and their temple. But differences between the old story and exilic conditions outnumbered similarities.

When a shift in international control brought the Persian Empire to power, Jews were permitted to return to Judah. But many understandably resisted leaving what had become a second home to return to a devastated city that only the oldest remembered. As Judeans searched the writings that were becoming their Scriptures, there seemed little precedent for changing direction so dramatically. In fact, some parts of Scripture seemed to indicate that they had lost Jerusalem through their own heedlessness and should not expect to regain it.

But a particular poet saw it differently, and penned the words found in Isaiah 43:16–19:

> The LORD,
>   who makes a way in the sea,
>   and a path in the mighty waters,
> who brings out chariot and horse,
>   army and warrior;
> they lie down and cannot rise,
>   they are extinguished, quenched like a wick—
> the LORD says, "Do not remember past events;
>   do not ponder ancient history.
> See, I'm doing something new;
>   now it sprouts up—don't you notice it?
> I'm making a way in the desert,
>   streams in the wilderness."

That farsighted writer glimpsed analogies between the exodus long before and the contemporary moment. The God who had long ago brought their ancestors across the Red Sea to a new homeland was also guiding events at hand. The God who overcame obstacles back then, who "made a way in the sea," could also make a way across the desert. The God who had given water to thirsty ancestors would provide what the exiles needed, both literally and spiritually. The return from Babylon was not the same as the exodus from Egypt. Where analogies could be drawn, the poet suggested that the audience "remember past events from long ago" (Isa. 46:9, AT). But where they could not, the poet suggested that precedent must be held loosely: "Do not remember past events; do not ponder ancient history. See, I'm doing something new." As a result of such prophetic insights, Jerusalem was reestablished, changing the course of Western history.

Ananias's Courage and Saul's Transformation

The book of Acts tells of an unprecedented event in the lives of two faithful Jews six centuries later, after Judaism had spread across the eastern Mediterranean world. One was Saul from Tarsus in southern Turkey. The other was Ananias, who lived in Damascus.

When Saul first heard the puzzling message being preached by others, a message highlighting the deeds, death, and reported resurrection of a teacher named Jesus, he reacted as many faithful people do to new ideas. He wanted to shut it down. Saul began a campaign of imprisoning and even killing fellow Jews who followed Jesus. Acts 9:1–9 relates his journey to further this work:

> Saul, still breathing threats and murder against the disciples of the Lord, went to the high priest and asked him for letters to the synagogues at Damascus, so that if he found any who belonged to the Way, men or women, he might bring them bound to Jerusalem. Now as he was going along and approaching Damascus, suddenly a light from heaven flashed around him. He fell to the ground and heard a voice saying to him, "Saul, Saul, why do you persecute me?" He asked, "Who are you, Lord? The reply came, "I am Jesus, whom you are persecuting. But get up and enter the city, and you will be told what you are to do." The men who were traveling with him stood speechless because they heard the voice but saw no one. Saul got up from the ground, and though his eyes were open, he could see nothing; so they led him by the hand and brought him into Damascus. For three days he was without sight, and neither ate nor drank.

The world as Christians know it has always been that in which Saul was stopped in his path. So it challenges our imaginations to see that day as it might have looked to him. What would it be like to pursue one course so zealously, only to learn that, sincere as you may have been, you were wrong? To learn that you must stop and do something else, now, without finishing the project?

Ananias was a Jewish follower of Jesus living in Damascus, the city where Saul intended to make his arrests. His predicament is even harder to imagine than Saul's:

> The Lord said to him in a vision, "Ananias." He answered, "Here I am, Lord." The Lord said to him, "Get up and go to the street called Straight, and at the house of Judas look for a man of Tarsus named Saul. At this moment he is praying, and he has seen in a vision a man named Ananias come in and lay his hands on him so that he might regain his sight." But Ananias answered, "Lord, I have heard from many about this man, how much evil he has done to your saints in Jerusalem; and here he has authority from the chief priests to bind all who invoke your name." But the Lord said to him, "Go, for he is an instrument whom I have chosen to bring my name before Gentiles and kings and before the people of Israel; I myself will show him how much he must suffer for the sake of my name." (Acts 9:10–16)

What mix of fear and anger, dread and hope must he have felt at the prospect of revealing himself to one who could have him imprisoned or killed? Once he has done this, would his family ever be safe again? Could he put others' lives at risk to help a violent person like Saul?

Saul waited on a street called Straight. Since individual roads are seldom named in Scripture, this one must have borne significance for the author, who had begun his narrative by quoting Isaiah's ancient words: " 'Prepare the way of the Lord, make his paths straight' " (Luke 3:4, quoting Isa. 40:3). Saul's zealous, well-intended, but violent path was about to make a U-turn for world history. With his leadership, the God of Abraham and Sarah, the God of Isaac and Rebekah, of Jacob and Leah and Rachel, and of Moses, that Jewish God would become the God of Gentiles too.

Christians can hardly imagine our history without this fundamental swerve in Saul. But it lay well beyond the expectations of earliest believers. At that moment the church's future hinged on frightened individuals being called to stop what they were doing and to do something else. Out of that moment came Saul's—that is, Paul's—creative and learned reinterpretations of the Hebrew Scriptures to make room for a theology of Jesus Christ, reinterpretations foundational for Gentile Christian self-understanding. In the days of both the exile and the early church, searching Scripture to find continuity between past and present changed the world.

As Jesus said, " 'Every scribe who has been trained for the kingdom of heaven is like the master of a household who brings out of his treasure what is new and what is old' " (Matt. 13:52). Modern people who look to ancient Scriptures for guidance find that they must both search the text and hear it anew. They do not romp down safe, well-worn, familiar paths, but look expectantly to find both old and new—what Scripture has been saying all along, whether we heard it or not, and what new word applies today.

This Book's Plan

History, including Western religious tradition, has been characterized by a human self-centeredness that has taken the rest of the earth for granted. But Scripture tells a different story, one in which human culture finds itself embedded within, and dependent upon, a larger cosmos that invites our respect and gratitude. Finding our way out of assumptions that are killing us into relationship with Creator and creation is crucial.

In chapter 2 we will read the creation story in Genesis 1 and consider our ties to other species and to the earth, our original vocation, and the kind of world the Bible's first chapter describes as our habitation. Care for the earth begins with grateful appreciation for its splendor.

Genesis 2–4 are filled with ecological language that we will examine in chapter 3. Both the deeds of Adam and Eve and those of their son Cain led to social alienation. They also led to alienation from the earth itself. According to these stories, what we do to one another directly affects our relationship to the ground from which our sustenance comes, and what happens to the ground determines our own life conditions.

In chapter 4 we will examine what Scripture says about human pride and its continued twisting of relationships. Humans imagine that we exist to take and gain. But we were made to give ourselves away. Ignoring God and God's creation, we find ourselves serving lesser things. The commodities that we have come to crave weigh us down, exacerbate injustices here and abroad, and degrade the earth with debris. To put human-made objects in their proper place as tools, we must learn the art of contentment.

Our relationship to the plant world will be discussed in chapter 5. Beginning with the manna in the wilderness and the food rules from Mount Sinai, we will examine contemporary agricultural practices. Some practices depend on cooperation from businesses and governments, but many can be adopted by communities, families, and individuals.

Chapter 6 concerns our relationship to animals. The Pentateuch prescribes a symbiosis between people and domestic beasts, and Scripture teaches respect for living creatures. Yet whole food systems today begin with the premise that neither animal suffering nor ecological degradation should stand in the way of human appetites. Changing our treatment of animals not only can answer biblical ethics but also can contribute to ecological and human health.

It is common in contemporary debates to pit social and ecological issues against one another. Quicker than one can say "spotted owl," caricatures replace reason and discussion is closed. Yet chapter 7 will argue that ecological health and human justice go hand in hand. Although the Bible has much to say about treatment of those who are economically weaker than ourselves, perhaps none speaks more clearly than Matthew 7:12, well known as the Golden Rule: "Do unto others as you would have them do unto you," or as farmer and writer Wendell Berry paraphrases, "Do unto those downstream as you would have those upstream do unto you."[3]

The Golden Rule spans not only space but time. Chapter 8 examines biblical injunctions to assure prosperity for our descendants. The notion that children should suffer from parents' sins is viewed as every bit as unjust today as it was then. In this chapter we will discuss how our generation is spending our children's ecological inheritance, especially by overusing fossil fuels.

The final chapter asks what kind of future Christians are building for. Apocalyptic preachers prefer worldwide, violent disasters that the faithful escape through "rapture" from the ruined planet. Such ideas lend themselves to ecological recklessness. Other visions of the future may be less entertaining, but are far more central to Scripture, such as the biblical virtue of moderation. Changes require not only creativity but courage, not only vision but gumption. Yet self-control is just what our tradition wisely teaches. The reward we may gain, what Jesus called "the pearl of great price," is the restoration of our good life on earth.

Each chapter includes not only questions for group and individual reflection but also practical suggestions for individuals and families to try at home. The notes and "For Further Reading" bibliography in the back of the book may also be of interest. Our own church's green team began its work by reading a book together. This study can help such groups, as well as adult classes and Bible study groups. Since each chapter grows from Scripture, the book could accompany a preaching and worship series. Key passages are listed in appendix A.

Questions for Thought and Discussion

1. What do you think are the greatest ecological challenges facing us today? What do you think are causes of concern? Reasons for hope?
2. What societal changes have you seen in your lifetime—changes you welcome? Changes you do not welcome? What factors make society able to change? What factors make it slow to change?
3. What heroes of cultural change do you admire most? What do you think enabled them to be more clear-sighted than others? How did they communicate their vision?

4. What biblical heroes do you admire? What is it like to imagine their own viewpoint on their circumstances and actions? What if Saul or Ananias had lacked sufficient courage?

5. Thinking ahead to the subjects of the rest of the study, what connections do you perceive between faith and ecological responsibility?

Try This at Home

For the next week, as you read the Bible or hear Scripture read in church, pay attention to what is said about creation, the earth, and its creatures. Try your hand at a little writing. It may be a poem, a prayer, or simply a list. Try putting on paper two things: first, the gifts of life that you cherish most, and second, what concerns you most about the state of the world. If you have children, you might consider inviting them to express their joys and concerns as well.

Also, for the next week, observe your news sources. How often do you find ecological problems raised? Who discusses them? On what basis? What do they commend?

The LORD is good to all,
  and God's compassion is over all that is made.
All your works shall give thanks to you, O LORD,
  and all your faithful shall bless you.
                                        —Psalm 145:9–10

We already know from experience with the "beautiful book"
of creation that this garden serves us. It serves us with good
foods, beauty, herbs, fiber, medicine, pleasant microcli-
mates, continual soil-making, nutrient processing, and seed
production. . . . Yet Genesis addresses *our* service to the garden. The garden's service *to us* is implicit; service *by us* to the
garden is explicit.
  —Calvin DeWitt, "Science, Scripture, and Con-serving
            Creation," in *Holy Ground: A Gathering of Voices
                                on Caring for Creation*

Chapter 2

Humans and Creation

Poetry

Many modern people read the Bible's first chapter as if it were a historical or scientific account of the earth's beginning. But listening to its rhythms and repetitions, we realize it is poetry. Read Genesis 1:1–2:3 out loud, listening as you read. If you are studying with others, read together the litany using this passage that is found in appendix B.

Certain refrains running throughout Genesis 1 establish its major themes: the repetitions "let there be . . . and there was . . ."; "and God saw that it was good"; "and there was evening, and there was morning." These phrases give structure to the passage. They also provide a framework for seeing God's relationship to the created world as this writer envisioned it. We will begin by unpacking each of these repeated phrases. Then we will discuss some of the particular claims made about humans on earth.

And God said, "Let there be . . . and there was . . ."
It is God who calls out to each part of creation, speaking it into being. This vision differs from that of other ancient stories that depicted creation arising from a battle among the gods. It differs also from Genesis 2, which shows God as a potter, shaping humans and animals as if with hands. Each of those accounts has

19

its place. But in Genesis 1, what is imagined is the divine voice that summons light, earth, and sky, all the vegetation and all the animals to emerge from the formless void. Each part of creation is summoned from the same undifferentiated, chaotic mass to its own place and vocation—the sea and its creatures no less than the humans. Each part responds immediately and directly to God's voice, becoming what God meant it to become.

"And God saw that it was good"

Though humans most often see creation's flaws, according to Genesis 1 God views it as fundamentally good. We know this phrase so well that we may overlook it. We may also overlook creation's majesty. We may go for long periods without looking at the color of the clouds or the ripples in the river, not really feeling the fur of animals who live with us, or the cool shelter under each tree. Then we get hungry—"nature deficit disorder," some call it—because the natural world feeds our souls. It is good, this earth that God made. Very good. Perhaps the poet envisions that creation satisfies God's sense of well-being as it does our own.

"And there was evening, and there was morning"

Setting aside questions such as whether a day means twenty-four hours and how long it really took for this teeming earth to come into being, here we note that time is an essential element in the earth's making. Even God takes time to let everything unfold. With time there is also rhythm. And there is plot. Through all these repeated phrases, we hear the increasing complexity of each day.

This story resembles Pachelbel's *Canon in D Major*, which starts out with a single, simple string of eight notes, then adds voice to voice, building in complexity, fervor, and reciprocity until the senses are almost overwhelmed. At that point the various voices stop intertwining and begin striking their notes together as if meeting up to come to rest—and then they do, resting at peace on their final chord.

Similarly here, on the first day light is all that happens, simply but profoundly. Without electric switches, matches, flints, or even stars, who but God could imagine, much less produce, such brilliance? Each day builds on the preceding as God first organizes and then populates the void, adding one being to another, building multiplicity. Light takes a whole day. But humans are postponed until day six, late in the afternoon, after land animals of all kinds. We enter the picture at its most intense moment, probably unnoticed at first among the crowds.

We humans, habitually anthropocentric, tend to think God saved the best for last. But if so, then Sabbath is greater even than humankind. Like light, the Sabbath rest gets a day all its own. There is a lovely painting by an unknown fifteenth-century artist (dubbed the Master of the Upper Rhine) called *The Garden of Paradise*. This painting does not, like so many, dwell on Adam and Eve eating the forbidden fruit. Instead, it shows eight people in various groupings enjoying what looks like Sabbath rest in a walled garden. One gathers fruit; another appears to be planting seeds; another plays with a child (Christ?); another, with angel wings, drowses while his companions chat. A woman in a splendid crown, perhaps Mary herself, contentedly reads a book, sharing the center of the painting with a table of food and drink. Flowers and trees surround them, each plant unique in its splendid detail. Birds, each likewise unique, rest on the wall and the trees. An artist's rendering of paradise, with all enjoying quiet rest. We can imagine the first Sabbath rest, not God's alone but that of the whole creaturely community, still dewy and bright in newness, perhaps still surprised to be there.

In God's Image

What does it mean to say that we humans are made in God's image (Gen. 1:26–27)? Theologians have argued this question for centuries. Some say it means that we are more like God than the rest of creation is. Yet the lines of distinction drawn even in Genesis 1 suggest that we are much more like the animals than like God. Like other land animals we are created on the sixth day. Like birds and fish we are blessed by God and told to multiply. Like all the animals we are given the plants for food.[1] As one theologian, Ruth Page, pointed out, "If God can accommodate in relationship the infinite qualitative distinction between the divine and the human, there is not much more to ask of the divine in accommodating the rest of creation."[2] She continues, "There is a relation between God and every creature analogous, in its own conditions, to one of love where human beings are concerned. . . . This divine-nature relationship makes possible the imaging of God in the natural as well as the human world."[3] Many who live close to animals see too many commonalities between us and them to deny their God-infused natures.

Yet the biblical writer specifies that humans are made in God's image, repeating it over and over as if to invite us to ponder its implications. Many have tried to identify some trait of God's that humans share, such as walking on two legs, as John Milton thought, or consciousness, language, reason, creativity, responsibility, or capacity to worship, as others have thought. The uniqueness of various human traits like these comes into question the more we know about animal species, however. Some say that to be made in God's image is to be male and female, a trait we share with many species, since verse 27 places "in the image of God" parallel with "male and female." Others suggest it means living in responsible relationship to God and other animals.[4] It is helpful to remember that this is not science, nor even theological proposition; it is poetry. Poetry can evoke possibilities without narrowing down to exclusive answers.[5]

Many scholars think the language may be drawing a contrast with practices of idolatry. In fact, the word translated as "image" here can in other contexts signify an idol (Num. 33:52; 2 Kgs. 11:18; Ezek. 7:20; Amos 5:26). In ancient Mesopotamia and Egypt, people often created idols in human forms, literally making God in their own image. Archaeologists working in the Middle East sometimes find it difficult to distinguish between statues of gods and statues of human worshipers. In some Christian traditions such as Eastern Orthodoxy and Roman Catholicism, icons and statues of Jesus and of the saints serve as reminders of the invisible divinity beyond them. Even in traditions of Protestantism that frown upon "graven images," most people still imagine God as a very large and old human, almost always white and male, failing to distinguish between God and the human-made images of God.

But here a reversal is suggested: Not that we make God in our image, but that God already made us in God's. We don't need statues or even mental pictures. Rather, to see God's image we look to other people whom we see reflecting this image most clearly. Do we see God in those who fashion themselves as masters of the universe? Or in those who display attributes commended by Jesus? If we want to be most like God, perhaps "godliness," rather than "playing God," is most suitable. And to complete the thought, we may see God's image reflected in nature as well.[6] To be made in God's image may well be to mirror God's priorities and intents.

Dominion

In light of humans' placement within the created world, parallel to other animals and sharing space and food with them, what should we make of the command in Genesis 1:28 to "have dominion"? This has been a point of contention, especially since the dawn of the ecological movement a generation ago. In 1967, medievalist Lynn Townsend White traced the history of Western exploitation of the nonhuman world, faulting Christian tradition, especially the theology of domination commonly justified by appeal to Genesis 1, for ever-increasing destruction of the world and its species. According to Christian tradition, he said, the rest of creation was explicitly given to humans for their use: "No item in the physical creation had any purpose save to serve man's purposes. And, although man's body is made of clay, he is not simply part of nature: he is made in God's image. Especially in its Western form, Christianity is the most anthropocentric religion the world has seen."[7]

Honest Christians will readily recognize these assumptions about our privileged place in the world. But as White noted, this attitude toward nature has not been universal in Christian tradition. Eastern Orthodox faith has not subscribed to it. So if only Western Christians seem to have read Genesis this way, we might wonder whether the problem lies with Scripture or with our tradition of interpretation.

Approaching this notion of dominion afresh, we might note first what is and is not included. Animals are named: fish, birds, cattle, wild animals, and creeping things. Plants are given as nourishment not just to humans but also to animals; everything that breathes shares this food supply. But if we are to believe the textual correction of verse 26 in the NRSV and NIV, the world's nonliving elements are not included.[8] The creation story does not authorize destruction of mountains, rivers, or coastlines, nor destruction of the habitats and food systems of other animals.

Second, the word is not "dominate" but "have dominion." More directly, according to the Hebrew, the command is "rule" (Tanakh, NIV; CEB suggests "take charge"). What a formidable prospect this must have been to earliest readers, who lacked the numbers and petroleum power we now take for granted. Humans were then, on the one hand, still relatively sparse and weak, subject to wild animals, drought, infertility, and disease. On the other hand, by the time this passage was written, domestic species had already been cultivated for thousands of years.

Biblical writers did not know how animal husbandry had developed. Earliest written records show humans already taking it for granted, and it is only recently that paleontologists have begun to reconstruct this process.[9] But Scripture's writers could not help noticing that they had inherited management of some other living beings. They were aware that this relationship between living beings was unusual: wolves, for instance, did not keep flocks of sheep as humans did, much as it might have been to their advantage. As our theological ancestors sought to explain the relationships they observed between themselves and others, they theorized that God must have assigned humans rule over at least some animals. Perhaps this writer imagined that in time we would domesticate all species. Indeed, Genesis 2:19–20 envisions the first human exercising the power of naming all animals domestic and wild, and Isaiah 11:6–9 (cf. 65:25) envisions wild and domestic animals, along with children, enjoying peaceful coexistence. At the same time, God's speeches in Job (chapters

38–41), which enumerate one animal species after another outside of human control and even knowledge, present a more realistic portrait of the way things are between humans and animals.[10]

While the command to exercise dominion may have simply reflected what Scripture's writers saw functioning, more recent people, increasingly divorced from the land, read into this verse an authorization that they adopted most readily, an authorization not to stewardship, but to exploitation. People who assume we are the most important creatures on earth can readily believe God made it all for our enrichment.

In ancient Judah a common metaphor for rule, both human and divine, was sheep tending. When we say with Psalm 23 "God is my shepherd, I shall not want," we are evoking the same metaphor used in Scripture for human dominion:

> God chose servant David,
>   and took him from the sheepfolds;
> from tending the nursing ewes God brought him
>   to be the shepherd of God's people Jacob,
>   of Israel, God's inheritance.
> With upright heart he tended them,
>   and guided them with skillful hand.
>   (Ps. 78:70–72)

Since both God's guidance and human kingship are modeled on human shepherding, dominion must mean something far different from exploitation. Rather, it means protection from exploitation, preservation of the flock from dangers that would diminish it, cultivation of a sustainable coexistence. We who have enjoyed the advantages of just government for the common good know that government's purpose is not simply to benefit those in charge. We do not take dominion in the human sphere to imply exploitation and depletion. Similarly if, as this writer thought, God had given humans responsibility to rule other animals, it is difficult to imagine how this verse could possibly have been intended to authorize exploiting, extracting, raping, pillaging, and using up everything within reach.

The Human Role

Immediately after the litany of creation's seven days, a second creation story appears in which God molds humans as a potter molds clay. The human vocation is described somewhat more specifically here than in Genesis 1. According to the NRSV, "The LORD God took the man and put him in the garden of Eden to till it and keep it" (Gen. 2:15). Other translations say, "to till it and to tend it" (Tanakh) or "to work it and take care of it" (NIV). The Hebrew word translated "till" here more often means "to work for someone, to serve," and even "to serve someone as a slave." The word translated "keep" means "to take care of, preserve, protect." We might translate this phrase regarding the human vocation as "to serve and preserve the garden."[11] Serving and preserving are polar opposites of exploitation and depletion. The fundamental first task assigned to humans is to assist the ground in carrying out its own vocation to be a garden, an orchard containing "every tree that is pleasant to the sight and good for food" (Gen. 2:9).

The description of the garden God planted, which humans are invited to serve and preserve, emphasizes not only its food value but also its aesthetic worth. Eden was a feast for both eyes and tongue (and, we may imagine, for nose and ears as well). Modern gardening tends to sever these two functions, creating inedible flower gardens around the house for beauty and maximizing land use on farms for efficiency, particularly that of large machinery. But in Eden, food was pleasant to see and the scenery was good for food, a happy place to serve.

Wendell Berry, who farms today in the same locale where he grew up as a child, noted the degradation of farmland over the years:

> I live in a part of the country that at one time a good farmer could take some pleasure in looking at. When I first became aware of it, in the 1940s, the better land, at least, was generally well farmed. The farms were mostly small and were highly diversified, producing cattle, sheep, and hogs, tobacco, corn, and the small grains; nearly all the farmers milked a few cows for home use and to market milk or cream. Nearly every farm household maintained a

garden, kept a flock of poultry, and fattened its own meat hogs. . . .

Now the country is not well farmed, and driving through it has become a depressing experience. Some good small farmers remain, and their farms stand out in the landscape like jewels. But they are few and far between, and they are getting fewer every year. The buildings and other improvements of the old farming are everywhere in decay or have vanished altogether. The produce of the country is increasingly specialized. The small dairies are gone. Most of the sheep flocks are gone, and so are most of the enterprises of the old household economy. There is less livestock and more cash-grain farming. When cash-grain farming comes in, the fences go, the livestock goes, erosion increases, and the fields become weedy.[12]

Like other critics of contemporary ecological practices, Berry contrasts the stewardship once common to knowledgeable farmers with extractive practices currently encouraged by farm policy and agribusinesses. Practices that degrade the land may still "till," but they no longer "keep"; they neither "serve" nor "preserve" the land. Such practices appear distant from what is envisioned in Genesis 1 and 2 as humans' role.

Each in Its Place

Psalm 104 celebrates many of the themes that Genesis 1 does. There each living thing inhabits its ecological niche:

> The trees of the LORD are watered abundantly,
>   the cedars of Lebanon that God planted.
> In them the birds build their nests;
>   the stork has its home in the fir trees.
> The high mountains are for the wild goats;
>   the rocks are a refuge for the coneys.
> You have made the moon to mark the seasons;
>   the sun knows its time for setting.
> You make darkness, and it is night,

when all the animals of the forest come creeping out.
The young lions roar for their prey,
    seeking their food from God.
When the sun rises, they withdraw
    and lie down in their dens.
People go out to their work
    and to their labor until the evening.

                                        (Ps. 104:16–23)

This is a harmonious world where all know their place. Even natural enemies cooperate in a timeshare that keeps both safe: the lions sleep in their beds before people rise from theirs. Humans are envisioned not as strangers set apart from the natural world, nor as observers studying the teeming world from some safe distance. Here we are every bit a part of the structure and rhythm of creation. As in Genesis 1, all these living beings, including the human beings, are surrounded and supported by structures that preceded them:

You stretch out the heavens like a tent,
    you set the beams of your chambers on the waters,
you make the clouds your chariot,
    you ride on the wings of the wind,
you make the winds your messengers,
    fire and flame your ministers.

You set the earth on its foundations,
    so that it shall never be shaken.
You cover it with the deep as with a garment;
    the waters stood above the mountains.
At your rebuke they flee;
    at the sound of your thunder they take to flight.
They rose up to the mountains, ran down to the valleys
    to the place that you appointed for them.
You set a boundary that they may not pass,
    so that they might not again cover the earth.

                                        (Ps. 104:2b–9)

The mountains and waters are not scenery for vacation admiration, but every living being's habitat, the world in which we are embedded, larger and more powerful than we, yet servants of God. Even wind, fire, and flood, terrifying elements of the natural world that humans know we cannot rule, are envisioned as God's messengers doing God's bidding, stopping at the places where God says, "Stop!"

Awe and Wonder

Unlike us, our scriptural ancestors could not ignore nature and its rhythms. Vulnerable to the elements, they were inescapably aware of both the earth's nonliving forces and its plants and animals. No electric lights by night, no central heating in winter, no skyscrapers, highways, or even sidewalks shielded them from immediate contact with darkness, cold and heat, wind and rough earth. But like Minnesotans who cope with winter by getting out and enjoying it, our ancestors who could not imagine separating themselves from their environment celebrated it:

> When I look at your heavens, the work of your fingers,
>   the moon and the stars that you have established;
> what are human beings that you are mindful of them,
>   mortals that you care for them?
>
> > (Ps. 8:3–4)

> The heavens are telling the glory of God;
>   and the firmament proclaims God's handiwork.
> > (Ps. 19:1)

Psalm 148 calls all created beings to praise. Beginning with highest heaven, the psalm enjoins angels, sun, moon, and shining stars to praise their creator. The earth, the monsters in the deep, the meteorological elements, the mountains and hills, fruit trees, wild and domestic animals, kings and subjects, men and women, old and young, are all told to praise God. Once again humans are not set in opposition to the natural world. Rather, they inhabit it alongside plants and animals. These psalms remind us that Scripture draws its greatest distinction not between humans and the rest of creation, nor even between living and nonliving beings—in fact, biblical Hebrew had no word for either "nature" or "culture"—but between the Creator and the rest of us, created ones who owe God service and praise.

Gratitude

Gratitude is a most appropriate response for us as inhabitants of this world, a home we neither bought nor paid for nor could ever have designed. In the same passage from Isaiah that invokes the exodus story discussed in chapter 1, plants, animals, and people are all named together. The plants display God's glory, while animals and humans, each in their own ways, respond to divine provision with praise:

> See, I'm doing something new;
> > now it sprouts up—don't you notice it?
> I'm making a way in the desert,
> > streams in the wilderness.
> The beasts of the field,
> > the jackals and ostriches, will honor me,
> for I have put water in the desert,
> > and streams in the wilderness
> to give water to my people,
> > my chosen ones,
> > this people whom I formed for myself,
> who will declare my praise.
> > > > (Isa. 43:19–21, AT)

We were intended to draw sustenance from creation's bounty. With each breath, we take in God's provision of air; with each drink, the precious water supply; with each bite of bread, the manna for one more day of love and service. We can begin to uphold the world that upholds us by recognizing these gifts with gratitude, especially our place in an ordered world that is full and fundamentally good, and our vocation to preserve the goodness and health of this living, teeming, exuberant world.

We have all received gifts for which sincere gratitude is difficult, gifts we awkwardly tuck away in drawers, gifts that inspire the verb "regifting." Perhaps only occasionally, we have received the one thing that took our breath away. The universe itself provides such gifts to those who pay attention.

One night recently, my husband and I took our annual pilgrimage to the country to sleep under the stars and watch for meteorites. We saw some, and they were splendid. But we also saw something we couldn't account for: an intensely bright star rising in the east as the sun was setting. We knew it wasn't Venus. Each time we woke throughout the night, the star had moved, until it faded low in the western sky as the sun rose. I told my astronomer father about it, and he confirmed what I suspected: it was Jupiter, the solar system's largest planet, closer to the earth than it had been since 1963.

The following night I got out a bird-watching scope. First I noticed with some surprise that the scope made many times more stars visible than my eyes could otherwise see. Despite the city glare, stars shone from every inch of blackness. I aimed the scope at the bright point we had watched throughout the previous night and gasped, beholding for the first time the white, white disk of Jupiter and, ranged on either side in a line like baby ducks, four small points of light, Jupiter's four largest moons, Io, Europa, Ganymede, and Callisto, the moons Galileo discovered in 1610. I have pulled out that scope for others since, who didn't believe it possible to be surprised enough to gasp, until they were. These kinds of divine gifts in the sky, in the trees, in the small creatures of earth and air, inspire us to rejoin the rest of the created world.

The astronauts who first viewed the earth from space saw something even more glorious than what we can find looking up from here. We have all seen photos of the swirling round sapphire of earth. Physician and poet Lewis Thomas provides this poignant description:

Viewed from the distance of the moon, the astonishing thing about the earth, catching the breath, is that it is alive. The photographs show the dry, pounded surface of the moon in the foreground, dry as an old bone. Aloft, floating free beneath the moist, gleaming, membrane of bright blue sky, is the rising earth, the only exuberant thing in this part of the cosmos. If you could look long enough, you would see the swirling of the great drifts of white cloud, covering and uncovering the half-hidden masses of land. If you had been looking for a very long, geologic time, you could have seen the continents themselves in motion, drifting apart on their crustal plates, held afloat by the fire beneath. It has the organized, self-contained look of a live creature, full of information, marvelously skilled in handling the sun.[13]

If we love this world, both its human and nonhuman parts, and if we love God, who created both us and all we see, and if we find pleasure in creation, we are already far along the road to considering our roles as inhabitants of the earth. Throughout this study we will examine how we might respond more mindfully to God's call to serve and to preserve this glorious land.

Questions for Thought and Discussion

1. What words or phrases in Genesis 1:1–2:3 stand out to you as particularly luminous? What do they mean to you?
2. What does "serving and preserving" the ground mean to you?
3. Where do you notice God's imprint in the world, whether human or nonhuman?
4. How would you describe the relationship between humans and animals? Between people and plants?
5. For what do you praise God? What causes you wonder and awe? Is there a particular discovery that you found moving?
6. How can people fill the vocation to tend the earth? Especially for those who are not farmers, what can such a vocation mean?

Try This at Home

Take some quiet time, preferably alone, to do nothing but observe some element of the created world. You might go outside or even into the woods or countryside. Or if the weather is uncomfortable, enjoy a window view or a book of photographs, or even the feel of a dog's or cat's fur. Don't look for words or evaluations, but simply take in the experience for at least twenty minutes, using all the senses you can. Afterward, tell someone else, or write down, what you noticed, what you thought, and what you felt.

The next day, do it again in a different place. Only this time, precede your contemplation with a prayer of gratitude for what you observed the day before. Caution: this practice can be addictive. However, it is good for your health.

If you have children, you might practice this exercise with them.

I placed the sand as a boundary for the sea,
    a perpetual barrier that it cannot pass;
though the waves toss, they cannot prevail,
    though they roar, they cannot pass over it.
But this people has a stubborn and rebellious heart;
    they have turned aside and gone away.
They do not say in their hearts,
    "Let us fear the LORD our God,
who gives the rain in its season,
    the autumn rain and the spring rain,
and keeps for us
    the weeks appointed for the harvest."
                                            —Jeremiah 5:22–24

One of the penalties of an ecological education is that one lives alone in a world of wounds. Much of the damage inflicted on land is quite invisible to laymen. An ecologist must either harden his [or her] shell and make believe that the consequences of science are none of his [or her] business, or must be the doctor who sees the marks of death in a community that believes itself well and does not want to be told otherwise.

                        —Aldo Leopold, *A Sand County Almanac,*
                        with Essays on Conservation from Round River

Chapter 3

Leaving the Garden

We saw in chapter 2 that Genesis imagines humans embedded in creation's order, yet given particular roles as custodians of the earth and its creatures. Biblical authors pay attention to human effects on the rest of creation and to its effect on us. Responses of awe, gratitude, and wonder such as we find in Scripture may well be our own first steps in renewing family ties with the rest of God's world.

In this chapter we'll read stories of unintended consequences. We will see parallels between human recklessness in the Genesis narratives and ecological alienation today, particularly the transgression of limits drawn by nature. We will envision reclaiming our lost place in what some have called the "great community," or "creation's web."

Christians and Jews remember the story of Eden. Many also remember the episode that follows, concerning the brothers Cain and Abel. We know that eating the forbidden fruit led to the first couple's alienation from God and from each other, and that Cain's murderous act deprived him of a brother and led him to leave God's presence. But alienation from the land itself, though detailed in these stories, has become obscure or even invisible to modern readers. The fact that ecological dimensions have been overlooked betrays cultural blindness. Passionist priest and cosmologist Thomas Berry points out the underlying problem:

It takes a universe to bring humans into being, a universe to educate humans, a universe to fulfill the human mode of being. More immediately, it takes a solar system and a planet Earth to shape, educate, and fulfill the human. The difficulty in recent times is that the concern of the human . . . has been focused almost exclusively on interhuman and divine-human relations. Human-Earth relations have not been given the comprehensive consideration needed. That is where our contemporary challenge is located.[1]

Genesis 2 and 3

The writer of Genesis 2:7 draws the closest possible connection between the human (*adam*) and the ground (*adamah*): the human is made from the dust of the ground. To make this verbal relationship clear in English, some have suggested that the *human* comes from *humus*, or the *earthling* from *earth*, or the *farmer* from *farmland*.[2]

In Genesis 2:19 God forms all animals and birds from this same humble soil. The word *adamah* ("ground," "land," or "soil") appears fourteen times in Genesis 2, 3, and 4, clearly signaling its centrality. Contemporary biology agrees with ancient theology. All life springs from plants' ability to draw nutrients from the ground and to turn them into growth for themselves and food for all animals, including humans. Even carnivores who eat herbivores ultimately depend on plants that depend on the soil.

Genesis 2:15 describes the human responsibility to till and keep, or serve and preserve, this ground in Eden. The first couple eats from Eden's bounty. They are given the trees in the garden for their food and are told to steer clear of one forbidden tree. But Genesis 3 narrates their transgression: of all the trees available, they choose this one.

We may wonder why God issued such seemingly arbitrary limits. What's the big deal about a piece of fruit? Unfortunately, if we look to the story for clues to God's reasons we can't find them.

After the serpent raises questions the couple never returns to God for clarification. The woman had started out most carefully, taking upon herself instructions originally given to her spouse, and stretching the command against eating into one against touching. But when the serpent contradicts God, she readily accepts his word. While the woman's moral reasoning ends by adding to the serpent's words her own rationalizations, her husband's moral reasoning never begins at all: when she gives him the fruit it goes straight to his mouth, no questions asked.

Later, "at the time of the evening breeze," God comes out for a stroll. Christians have traditionally heard God's question "Where are you?" as an accusation. But perhaps God is simply reconnecting, as family members do at day's end. The couple's attempt to hide signals their alienation even before God perceives what has happened. God's speech details ruptures between them and the serpent and between the two of them. But the largest portion, in fact the climax of the whole speech, belongs to their alienation from the ground itself:

> "Cursed is the ground [*adamah*] because of you;
>   in toil you shall eat of it all the days of your life;
> thorns and thistles it shall bring forth for you;
>   and you shall eat the plants of the field.
> By the sweat of your face
>   you shall eat bread
> until you return to the ground [*adamah*],
>   for out of it you were taken;
> you are dust,
>   and to dust you shall return."
>
> (Gen. 3:17b–19)

Biblical scholar Ellen Davis tells of a group of farmers with whom she studied Genesis 3. Though theologically untrained, they noted what any Israelite would have seen, which she and her urban students had missed: when humans are disconnected from God, the soil is the first to suffer.[3] She observed that the thorns and thistles God said would grow outside of Eden are signs of desiccated, eroded land—land that has been mistreated.

But there is more here. As another biblical scholar, Brigitte Kahl, has pointed out, "until you return to the ground" holds a double meaning:

> The "back to the earth" of Gen. 3:19 has been almost exclusively remembered at the tombs of the dead. Its challenge to Christian life practices was seldom heard. But the text very explicitly talks about a change of direction, for the Hebrew word for *return* implies also the theological dimension of repentance, turning back to God.[4]

The wording implies that one day humans may rethink our actions and return to the ground, to our original vocation to serve the land.

Even though all has changed, the narrator repeats words from Genesis 2, saying: "The LORD God sent him forth from the garden of Eden, to till [again, "serve"] the ground from which he was taken" (v. 23). To protect the man and woman from further temptation, God replaces the moral boundary they had transgressed with a physical one, exiling them from the garden and blocking access. Overstepping their limits regarding the earth's fruit led not to closer connections but to alienation, because the earth's bounty is not to be received on human terms alone.

What might God have said, had they asked more questions? Working as a secretary in my early twenties, I wanted to know the "why" and "how" of assignments. My first manager accused me of excessive curiosity. I fared better when a different boss allowed me to work for a day in each department to better understand the whole. Which kind of manager would God have been had the first couple taken the time to understand instructions? Unfortunately, this conversation is short-circuited by their failure to inquire. Unintended consequences quickly follow this reckless act. They do not die, not immediately. But they do lose their home, and find themselves exiled from the garden and alienated from God, from each other, and from the soil.

Limitless Use of Resources

God's having set one tree off-limits may seem arbitrary. But it should come as no surprise that, just as the sea and land have their defining boundaries, human life also involves limits. Laws of nature impose physical limitations on every being, including ourselves. But there are many things that natural laws allow us to do that are nevertheless harmful. Ancient statutes in the Pentateuch set scores of restrictions, saying for instance, "You shall not kill; you shall not steal; you shall not commit adultery; you shall not covet," but not "you shall not fly," since laws forbid only what we *can* do. In most spheres of human life a significant difference reigns between what we are capable of doing and what we wisely should do. Committing felonies, violating trust with other people, and mistreating our bodies all lead to consequences most individuals would prefer not to face: when it comes to law, society, and health, "may" and "can" clearly don't coincide. But there is a widespread assumption that humans may do to creation whatever we can do, especially if it benefits us economically.

One of many everyday acts of limitlessness is waste of electricity, an action bearing consequences hidden from most eyes. In many countries in the developing world, homes and businesses equipped for electricity experience regular rolling blackouts known as "load shedding." Where demand exceeds supply, electricity is rationed throughout the network to prevent power stations from shutting down and to keep hospitals and government offices running. Nepal, for instance, has tremendous untapped hydroelectric potential, but because of poverty and governmental inefficiency, its urban citizens regularly find themselves in the dark, often fourteen to sixteen hours a day, while many rural areas lack electricity altogether. While Nepalis find creative adaptations, it's hard to run a business with daily power outages. Experts fear that as populations grow in number and wealth worldwide, nonrenewable resources are depleted, and severe weather increases, load shedding will spread.

Americans tend to treat power as if it were limitless. Nearly half of all electricity in the United States comes from coal extracted from the earth. We do not see the coal that fuels our electricity-rich lifestyle; we only see the lights, blow-dryers, and central air conditioning systems powered by this mineral. Many don't view leaving a TV running in an empty room all day as an ethical issue. At most it may hurt the pocketbook.

Despite national and state incentives to conserve, our usage continues to grow. On a recent tour of model homes I saw sign after sign touting the energy efficiency of new 4500-square-foot houses, many of them equipped with five or six large televisions and at least two full-sized refrigerators, causing me to wonder what the signs could possibly have meant.

The impact from home to home is cumulative. In Indiana where I live, for instance, an average of 62 pounds of coal are mined, processed, and burned every day for each individual.[5] This means that the average family of four consumes ninety half-ton pickup loads of coal every year—in our homes, on the city streets, in stores and offices.

Having several tons of coal burned for us each year is not cost-prohibitive for most. But our bills don't cover the full expense of mining, transporting, burning, and using the coal. In October 2009, the National Research Council released a report describing the externalized damage (that is, costs not paid by producers and consumers) to ecological and human health from fuels used in America.[6] Some of these damages are paid by taxpayers when corporations neglect environmental cleanup. Most of the damages, however, are not the kind money can repair. Other people bear some costs: miners' deaths and injuries; destruction of homes and property for mountaintop removal; and health damages from exposure to power plant emissions such as arsenic, lead, and mercury. Still other damage—the destruction of streams, forests, and wildlife habitats—is borne by the land itself and its nonhuman inhabitants, as well as by future generations. Government, industry, and many citizens know about these externalized damages. Yet they continue.[7]

Electricity use involves relatively low-tech tampering with ecological and human health. But the notion of limitlessness also infuses product development in increasingly complex ways that affect us all. For instance, the assumption is widespread that because government regulation of some products exists, anything sold in the United States—body care products, cleaning fluids, genetically modified seeds and foods—must have been found safe. Yet most remain untested, and others containing known carcinogens, hormone disruptors, and neurotoxins are marketed with little regulation. For many, contents need not be disclosed.

It is not as if we haven't experienced regret before over human tampering. From the well-intended introduction of invasive nuisances such as kudzu in 1876 and starlings in 1890, to the lethal exposure of humans to radioactivity during nuclear testing, we've seen repeated evidence of the risks of transgressing bounds without considering whether expected gains are worth uncertain and often unwanted consequences. As will be discussed later in this chapter, tampering with ecological balance in the Plains States led to the topsoil loss known as the Dust Bowl of the 1930s, whose effects remain today. Limitless exploitation and manipulation of the natural world has become our era's forbidden fruit, reached for because we can, increasing our knowledge at the expense of our wisdom, and often degrading or destroying our own habitat. Like Adam and Eve, we trade the garden for thorns and thistles.

Genesis 4

Alienation from the ground becomes even more pronounced in the story of the next generation. Here for the first time the word "sin" appears. Once again, ruptures among humans and between humans and God are much more widely recognized than the ecological ruptures.

After Eve bears Cain and his brother Abel and they grow to adulthood, Cain is found following the vocation set out for humans as tiller of the earth. Why Abel keeps sheep instead of farming land is not stated. This is puzzling: until this point humans have only been authorized to eat plants. It will save us from much misdirection to note that it is Cain, and not his brother, who carries on the family business bequeathed by God.

In fact, Cain is the first to offer God a gift from his harvest. No sacrifices had been commanded. For all we know from the story, this expression of gratitude is Cain's own invention. Perhaps following his brother's example, Abel brings an offering from the flock. Inexplicably, God "had regard for (or as the Hebrew says, "gazed upon") Abel and his offering," but did not show the same regard for Cain and his gifts.

Interpreters through the ages have been sidetracked by this moment, thinking God could not have behaved unfairly, so fault must be found with Cain. Perhaps, even though no sacrifices have yet been commanded, and though sacrifices would later include fruit and grain along with meat, Cain should have known God would prefer lambs over limes and lima beans. Perhaps, some suggest—though the story does not say this—Cain didn't offer the best of his fruit. Perhaps, others suggest—though the story does not say this either—Cain gave his offering with bad intentions. Those who seek to blame Cain for God's behavior fall into the role of Job's unhelpful friends, blaming Job for the disasters that God admits to having unjustly authorized (Job 2:3). We are better off simply noting the story's realism: life is inexplicably unfair, and siblings often struggle with unequal blessings.

The lesson God evidently wishes Cain to absorb is simple but crucial. As Jesus would later affirm, it is not what goes into people that defiles them but what comes out (Matt. 15:11, 18). What happens to us, even what is unjust, passes through our experience and is gone; it does not mar who we are. It is rather what comes out of us, what we say and do in response to painful events, that can make us sinners or saints. What happens to Cain is unfair but momentary; what he does with it determines who he is. God counsels Cain to resist the anger rising within him, or in God's own words, to control the wild beast that is crouched at Cain's door, ready to spring and devour him (4:7). Like his parents before him, Cain bears responsibility to choose well.

No one up to this point has enjoyed more explicit moral teaching than Cain does, hearing the alternatives God outlines. But he declines to respond. Instead he invites his brother to the field and kills him, spilling his blood on the fertile ground. As he repeatedly refuses to take responsibility, stonewalling and blaming God instead, the man who destroyed his only brother alienates himself from God. But what is emphasized above all in God's words to Cain, like those to his parents, is his broken relationship to the land. Killing his brother, he has polluted the soil and dissipated its fruitfulness:

> And the LORD said, "What have you done? Listen; your brother's blood is crying out to me from the ground [*adamah*]! And now you are cursed from the ground [*adamah*], which has opened its mouth to receive your brother's blood from your hand. When you till the ground [*adamah*], it will no longer yield to you its strength; you will be a fugitive and a wanderer on the earth." (Gen. 4:10–12)

In two generations the fruitful covenant between humans and the earth is broken. The taking of forbidden fruit in the garden transgresses against divinely imposed limitations. This seemingly innocent act leads to the unintended consequence of exile from the garden to a much more arduous life. It also leads, in the next generation, to jealousy and violence. Within two more chapters it leads to limitless wrongdoing: "Every inclination of the thoughts of their hearts was only evil continually" (6:5). The first large-scale ecological disaster results, a flood that nearly renders land animals and people extinct.

When we do wrong, others suffer in unexpected, unpredictable ways. The land and its creatures suffer from our deeds as well. It is the quality of the soul that is at stake in Genesis 3 and again in Genesis 4. It is also the quality of the soil. Though they were not scientists in the modern sense, our ancestors understood ecological dimensions of human action. Unfortunately, every generation since Cain has continued his pattern, competing violently for advantage, for blessing, for land itself, failing to see that our alienation from one another defiles the ground that is our source and home. The Rev. Pat Watkins, a Methodist missionary and pastor, explains:

The problem is not that we have no Biblical or historical traditions of creation care; the problem is that our isolation from God's creation makes us read the Bible with blinders on. As we study the scriptures, we simply miss the richness that is right in front of us because God's creation is no longer on our radar screens. To put it another way, we're not looking through the lens of creation. It's not that we've become bad people; we're just not aware of all the Bible has to say on this subject, because we're not looking for it. And we don't look for it because we've lost our connection to the natural world.[8]

Becoming Native to This Place

Adam and Eve were sent from their home to live outside the garden, and Cain lost both home and vocation to become a restless, rootless wanderer. Given the losses of home that characterize these originating stories, perhaps it is not surprising how many ecologically themed books include this word "home" in their titles. A glance at my own bookshelf yields: Gary Paul Nabhan's *Coming Home to Eat*, Kelly Cone and Erik Knutzen's *The Urban Homestead*, Wendell Berry's *Home Economics*, Edward Abbey's *The Journey Home*, and several volumes titled with such words as "community," "place," and "local." One of these, Wes Jackson's *Becoming Native to This Place*, a little book of essays centered on the history and present state of agriculture in Kansas, reads in interesting ways alongside the Genesis stories.

Jackson, a geneticist and founder of the Land Institute, begins by asking why 25,000 Native Americans were able to prosper in a county whose white population has declined ever since. Researching the history of one eighty-acre tract, he found that in seventy years, fourteen white families became impoverished there, unable to thrive because they didn't know the land, its characteristics, and its needs. Jackson recounts buying an abandoned house and finding three inches of topsoil weighing down the ceiling, blown up from surrounding fields in the Dust Bowl.[9] This severe loss of soil during the drought of 1930–1936 was caused by farmers' having removed the perennial prairie grass whose roots anchored the soil, and having substituted annual crops ill-suited to that habitat.[10]

At a recent meeting in northern Kentucky, Jackson displayed a banner thirty feet tall, showing the depth of roots of perennial grains, next to the incomparably thinner and shorter annual roots that must begin every year from seeds. Learning from the prairie led him to develop perennial crops that, like fruit trees, sustain themselves and supply food without yearly replanting. Jackson takes his cues from the first-century BCE Roman poet Virgil, who spoke of limitations the wise impose on themselves by observing the natural world:

> Before we plow an unfamiliar patch
> It is well to be informed about the winds,
> About the variations in the sky,
> The native traits and habits of the place,
> What each locale permits, and what denies.[11]

This is only one example of the conversation that Jackson says we must have with nature itself, learning in each locale what the nonhuman world, over the course of hundreds of millennia, has learned grows best, rather than forcing the land to do what it is not made to do. Quoting Francis Bacon's dictum that we must "bend nature to our will," Jackson responds, "The agricultural assumption that nature is to be either subdued or ignored is embedded in a larger cultural assumption," that is, the economic paradigm of extractive consumerism, the assumption that it is acceptable to use every means possible to take all that we desire from the earth, a practice that impoverishes the land and imperils its use by future generations. "Rather than ask what nature requires of us here, we mostly ask what we can get away with. The latter is a childish question."[12] Though the analogies are clear, Jackson is not thinking about the Genesis story, but rather the history of Western civilization, when he says, "Since our break with nature came with agriculture, it seems fitting that the healing of culture begin with agriculture."[13]

Other Passages

Genesis is not the only place that scriptural writers draw attention to ecological dimensions in our actions. In a passage observing the upending of many of the Ten Commandments, the prophet Hosea saw the entire nonhuman world languishing over human faithlessness:

> There is no faithfulness or loyalty,
>   and no knowledge of God in the land.
> Swearing, lying, and murder,
>   and stealing and adultery break out;
> bloodshed follows bloodshed.
> Therefore the land mourns,
>   and all who live in it languish;
> together with the wild animals
>   and the birds of the air,
>   even the fish of the sea are perishing.
>   (Hos. 4:1b–3)

The same Hebrew word that means "mourns" also means "dries out" or "withers." Whereas humans mourn with tears, the ground here mourns in drought. Both become weakened. Using terminology very similar to both the Hosea passage above and the story of Cain, Isaiah 24:4–6 claims:

> The earth dries up and withers,
>   the world languishes and withers;
>   the heavens languish together with the earth.
> The earth lies polluted
>   under its inhabitants;
> for they have transgressed laws,
>   violated the statutes,
>   broken the everlasting covenant.
> Therefore a curse devours the earth,
>   and its inhabitants suffer for their guilt;

therefore the inhabitants of the earth dwindled,
   and few people are left.

Here it is not simply the ground that suffers but the entire earth, the world, and the heavens—the whole cosmos—when humans overstep our bounds, when we violate one another and misuse our gifts of intelligence and choice.

Earlier translations of verse 5 had the earth "defiled" by its inhabitants, rather than "polluted," drawing attention to creation's sacredness. The RSV's use in 1952 of the word "polluted" drew out a more literal dimension of this defilement. Especially after the appearance of Rachel Carson's 1962 book *Silent Spring*, which explored the unforeseen destruction wrought by agricultural use of DDT, awareness has grown that human activity indeed pollutes our land—and also our water and air—much more quickly and permanently than previously imagined. We began to discover, in the words of Isaiah 24:5, the laws, statutes, and covenants governing the natural world as a closed but sustainable system within which humans must learn to live. The apocalyptic picture in these verses of a curse devouring the earth, inhabitants dwindling in number, crops failing, cities reverting to chaos, and desolation abounding, sounds like science fiction. But throughout the Hebrew Scriptures, "land degradation is a sure sign that humans have turned away from God. Conversely, the flourishing of the land marks a return to God. In short, the Old Testament represents the condition of the land as the single best index of human responsiveness to God."[14]

In Genesis 3, unbounded desire for what humans are capable of taking, but are warned not to take, results in alienation, removing people from the harmonious community of relative freedom to a place outside of Eden, a place of alienation and hardship. In the next generation, such unbounded desire gives birth to jealousy, impulsiveness, violence, lying, boundless anxiety, and finally homelessness and rootlessness. What if we could ask these distant, mythic ancestors Adam and Eve, living lives they weren't born for, in the land of exile, one son killed and the other a killer, "Was it worth it for that fruit?" What kind of similar questions will our descendants ask us?

Creation's Web

Liberty Hyde Bailey said early in the twentieth century, "To live in right relation with his natural conditions is one of the first lessons that a wise farmer or any other wise man learns."[15] It is time to regain our vision for humanity's relationship to the rest of the world. Philosophers and theologians from Aristotle until the age of scientific dominance spoke in various ways of the "Great Chain of Being," in which all that exists is interlinked, from God and the angels to inanimate rocks. Charles Darwin compared the interrelatedness of life with "an entangled bank" comprised of varieties of plants, birds, insects, and worms, "so different from each other, and dependent on each other."[16] Nineteenth-century naturalist John Muir observed that the human, who has "flowed down through other forms of being and absorbed and assimilated portions of them into himself, [is] a microcosm most richly Divine because most richly terrestrial."[17] Theologian Ruth Page speaks of creation as a web, saying, "Not only is a web a pattern of interconnection, but when one part shakes, it all shakes."[18] These images express creation's interwovenness. They hold out the hope that, when humans learn our place and limits, we will live more harmoniously with the world that surrounds and supports us.

In Romans 8, the apostle Paul likewise draws a close connection between human activity and the cosmos. He describes all of creation waiting with eager anticipation, the whole world "groaning in labor pains" on our account. The J. B. Phillips translation is especially poignant:

> In my opinion whatever we may have to go through now is less than nothing compared with the magnificent future God has in store for us. The whole creation is on tiptoe to see the wonderful sight of the [children] of God coming into their own. (Rom. 8:18–19)

In other words, "The whole created world is longing for Homo sapiens, the creature that dares to call itself 'wise,' to become fully human."[19]

What might it mean to know better our place in creation's web, to exchange an anthropocentric worldview for one attentive to a world that does not shout for our attention but, though surrounding us on all sides, whispers so softly that amid the human din we must tune up our eyes and ears? Can we see the white oak's most subtle spring flowering among screaming billboards, or hear the call of the red-winged blackbird over the imperious din of traffic? Some of us were fortunate enough to have been nurtured by parents who taught us these things, but for most of us, meeting the nonhuman world is an act of reclamation. I remember my own chagrin when attempting to teach my shreds of hard-won knowledge of tree identification to Fletcher Podoko, a student from Malawi. After patiently attending to my descriptions of compound and simple leaves, alternate, opposite, palmate, and pinnate, he responded as if I were introducing him to people by the shapes of their noses: "In Malawi we don't talk about categories. We just know our trees. Don't Americans know their trees?"[20] Since trees are not my native language, I need the verbal clues until fluency grows.

Science writer Hannah Holmes spent a year entranced by exquisite detail when she studied the inhabitants of her own yard in suburban Maine, learning—and teaching readers—the habits of creatures most of us look past every day: intelligent crows, sociable chipmunks, industrious worms, hidden nematodes.[21] Biologist Stacy O'Brien tells the remarkable story of a barn owl who lived his whole life as her companion, disclosing details of barn owl behavior unknown to those who studied them in the wild.[22] Microbiologist Ursula Goodenough explains the intricacies of life's origins and organization, drawing lessons of awe along the way.[23] These and many other keen observers of nonhuman life join previous generations of writers—Henry David Thoreau, John Muir, Aldo Leopold, Rachel Carson—who called attention to a remarkable world ever present beyond the human. If travel to foreign lands enlarges our sense of the world's breadth, all the more do the smallest expeditions—to plant an asparagus crown in the dirt; to observe a honey bee's path—remind us not to leave our relationship to the earth in its tattered state, but with humility to reclaim our place in the web of creation.

Questions for Thought and Discussion

1. What implications do you see when reading Genesis 2–4 with attention to the frequency of the word *adamah* ("ground" or "soil")? What does it mean to "return to the ground" in a constructive way?

2. What is your gut-level reaction to the idea of living within legal, social, and religious limitations? What is your reaction to the idea of living within ecological limits? What examples come to mind?

3. What instances have you seen of competition or greed leading to human violence against other humans? Do you think it is appropriate to speak of human violence in relation to animals? To plants? To inanimate parts of nature such as soil or mountains? What is human responsibility in these relationships?

4. Consider your home, church, or town. Do you observe instances in which electricity or gas are being burned without benefit (i.e., wasted)?

5. What are some ways individuals and churches can seek to regain a sense of being part of the "web of creation"?

Try This at Home

Begin a record of monthly energy use in your home or church. If possible, start it from a year ago. Chart the month, amount used, cost, and if possible the average temperature, which is included in some bills. Then perform an energy audit. Some power companies or renewable energy dealers will do this for free, pointing out ways to conserve costs. If you cannot find an auditor, look online to learn issues to watch for. Here is a starting place: http://energy.gov/home-energy-audits.

Make a list of changes you can make. Check on whether your state, city, or national government or utility company offers help financing the change. Prioritize the least expensive and easiest changes, and make a monthly budget of time and money. The first may simply be to turn off what is not being used. As you make changes, note the decreases in energy use.

If you have a family or roommates, make it a game: who can find new ways to conserve? How much fossil fuel does this change represent?

You have made us for yourself, O Lord, and our heart is restless until it rests in you.

—Saint Augustine, *Confessions of Saint Augustine*

How do we begin to know this earth and so regain that reverence for life that leads to change? The first step in this process is to recognize that we are an integral part of all that is, not superior beings for whom everything else is there to be used. We are woven into the "web of the universe," and nothing we do is without significance to the rest.

—Elizabeth J. Canham, "Simplicity," in *Heart Whispers: Benedictine Wisdom for Today*

Chapter 4

Commerce and Contentment

Two Alternatives

In chapter 3 we explored alienation from God, one another, and the earth—in short, from God and God's world. God had challenged Cain to escape the bondage of rage. When Cain refused, the result was not freedom, but bloodshed, recrimination, and restless wandering. Beyond the two alternatives of doing right and being enslaved to destructive impulses there was no third option.

The first of the Ten Commandments puts the alternatives starkly: I am the LORD your God, who brought you out of slavery; do not worship other gods (Exod. 20:2–3). The second commandment prohibits the manufacture and worship of idols, human-made gods (vv. 4–5). Again the alternatives are starkly put: We can choose to worship other gods, often in the form of manufactured idols, or we may worship the God who liberates from bondage. Jesus similarly drew an either/or distinction: "No one can serve two masters. . . . You cannot serve God and wealth" (Matt. 6:24). In a culture that knew too well the ubiquity of masters on all levels from the household to the empire, Jesus had no need to say, "And don't even think you can avoid serving any masters at all!"

Modern ideas about individual freedom can deceive us into imagining ourselves as masters of our fate and captains of our

53

soul. But according to Scripture such independence does not exist. Refusal to live in God's ways leads not to independence but to slavery to another taskmaster. As we will discuss in this chapter, material wealth has become a powerful god in our culture, not serving our benefit but rather cajoling our society into unsustainable and surprisingly unhappy lifestyles. In recognizing this human-made god and its empty promises for what they are, we free ourselves to rejoin the infinitely more compelling world that God has made.

Biblical Visions of Pride and Idolatry

Scripture often characterizes those who resist God as proud and arrogant. In Psalm 10, these character traits go hand in glove with greedy exploitation of the poor:

> Why, O LORD, do you stand far off?
>   Why do you hide yourself in times of trouble?
> In arrogance the wicked persecute the poor—
>   let them be caught in the schemes they have devised.
>
> For the wicked boast of the desires of their heart,
>   those greedy for gain curse and renounce the LORD.
> In the pride of their countenance the wicked say, "God will not
>   seek it out";
>   all their thoughts are, "There is no God."
>
> (vv. 1–4)

The irony of such arrogance, according to Scripture, is that those who lift themselves too high will inevitably fall. The book of Proverbs frequently associates pride with greed and ultimate downfall, most famously in this saying:

> Pride goes before destruction,
>   and a haughty spirit before a fall.
> It is better to be of a lowly spirit among the poor
>   than to divide the spoil with the proud.
>
> (16:18–19)

Isaiah's second chapter presents one of the Bible's most complex and vivid studies of human pride and its associated sins. The proud and "lifted up" are ironically depicted as bowing low to idols, idols their own hands made. In this poem we can see correlations between the idols of Isaiah's time and those of our own.

The chapter consists of two parts of unequal length. Both parts involve the nations coming to Judah, and both involve weapons of war. Both depict humankind in the act of worship, whether of God or of idols. The first and shorter portion, in which the nations turn their swords into plowshares, is by far the better known. We will return to that section later. But first we will examine Isaiah 2:6–21, which follows that famous vision. It connects pride inexorably with both idolatry and desperation. The passage is long but vivid and filled with repetition:

> For you have abandoned your people,
>   house of Jacob,
> for they are full of sorcerers from the east
>   and fortune tellers like the Philistines,
>   and they clasp hands with foreigners.
> Their land is filled with silver and gold,
>   and there is no end to their treasures.
> Their land is filled with horses,
>   and there is no end to their chariots.
> Their land is filled with idols—
>   they bow down to the work of their hands,
>   to what their own fingers have made.
>
> And humanity will be brought down;
>   each person laid low—do not lift them up!
> Go into the rock, and hide yourself in the dust
>   from the terror of the LORD,
>   and from the splendor of God's majesty!
> People's proud eyes will be brought down,
>   and humanity's haughtiness laid low,
> and the LORD alone will be exalted on that day.

For the day of the LORD of hosts
    is upon all that is proud and haughty,
    and upon all that is lofty and high,
upon all the cedars of Lebanon, high and lofty,
    and upon all the oaks of Bashan,
and upon all the high mountains,
    and upon all the lofty hills,
and upon every tall tower,
    and upon every fortified wall,
and upon all the ships of Tarshish,
    and upon all the lovely boats.

People's pride will be brought down,
    and human haughtiness laid low.
    The LORD alone will be exalted on that day,
and the idols will completely pass away.
And they will go into rocky caves
    and dusty holes
before the terror of the LORD
    and the splendor of God's majesty
    arising to overawe the earth.
On that day people will throw away
    to the moles and to the bats
their gods of silver and gods of gold
    which they made for themselves to worship.
They will hide in clefts of rocks
    and crevices of cliffs
before the terror of the LORD
    and the splendor of God's majesty
arising to overawe the earth.

                                    (Isa. 2:6–21, AT)

The first few verses show the nations filling Judah and leading it astray. Innumerable weapons of war—horses and chariots—bring no security. Silver and gold litter the land. But all these things usher in not freedom but slavery: "they bow down to the work of their hands, to what their own fingers have made."

The poem then introduces a nightmarish vision that plays with the theme of bowing down. Though humans have just been depicted as bowing before idols, here they are seen as proud and arrogant toward God. They are so "proud and lofty" that they are compared to the great trees of Lebanon and Bashan that ancient emperors logged for profit, and to other mighty structures both natural and human. But a relentlessly repetitive litany depicts the defeat of all that stands tall. In the end, human idolaters flee from God, tossing aside as scattered debris all that they cherished most.

True Love of Self and God

What is this connection in Scripture between idolatry and prideful resistance to God, between hauteur and self-humiliation? Theologian R. R. Reno makes use of Saint Augustine's discussion of self-love to answer this question. For Augustine, to turn one's back on God is to attempt to make the self one's central concern. To do so is a mistake, Reno says:

> No false love can be successful, because it has no place, no truth, in which to come to rest. This is true of every misguided love. We can try to make ourselves happy with wealth, but neither the luster of coins nor their ability to bring us all the merchant's cargo is powerful enough to bring us peace. . . . All the more so with pride: it can evacuate the soul of love of God, but it cannot fill us with self-love, for the self has nothing to offer itself other than the capacity to glorify God.[1]

Both pride and idolatry arise from the same mistake of denying what we were made to be. They lead to the same sad conclusion, the inability to find satisfaction elsewhere:

> While we may attempt, in pride, to make ourselves our own ground and the source of our own happiness, we cannot succeed, for we have nothing to give ourselves other than our reality as creatures whose true happiness is in God alone. . . .

> Pride will fail, and in failing, it becomes not its opposite,
> which is humility, but instead the perversion of a perversion,
> the redoubled futility of slavery to idols of our own fabrica-
> tion.[2]

In other words, just as misuse of the created world for purposes for which it was not intended yields ecological crisis, so,
according to Augustine as read by Reno, misuse of ourselves for
purposes for which we were not made leaves a personal and social
vacuum: "The inevitable slide from pride to idolatry should not
surprise us," Reno comments. "We are made for love, and our
desire is to give ourselves away, not to draw in upon ourselves
as the source and ground of our happiness. . . . Pride's project of
finding rest in the self will always find concrete expression as the
worship of idols."[3]

The view of pride reflected in Isaiah, in Augustine, and in
Reno's discussion takes this attitude seriously. Pride is not simply a miffed arrogance, an upturned nose, a social slight, a too-
certain intellectual stance. Rather, pride is Cain's leaving the
loving, beckoning God. To dethrone God is not to enthrone ourselves—though it may be what we intend—but rather to enslave
ourselves to lesser gods, false gods.

Neuroscientist Patrick McNamara similarly noted that the
self is not a thing but a process: fragile, transient, always in flux.
"When it attaches itself to unworthy objects," he said, "slavery
is the result. When, however, it lets go of these attachments and
instead yokes itself up with God, illumination and freedom are
the result."[4]

Seeking God

The first part of Isaiah 2 tells a different story. Its vision contrasts
sharply with the passage concerning idols that follows it. In verses
2–4, the nations likewise come to Judah. But here they come not
to bring their own wares and messages, but to be instructed.
Finding peace in God, they reshape their own weapons into tools
for carrying out humans' vocation to tend the earth:

In days to come
   the mountain of the Lord's house
will be established at the peak of the mountains,
   and will be lifted up above the hills,
and all the nations will stream to it.
   and many peoples will come, and they will say,
"Come, let us go up to the mountain of the Lord,
   to the house of the God of Jacob,
that we may be taught God's ways,
   so we may walk in God's paths."
From Zion will come teaching,
   and the word of the Lord from Jerusalem.
God will judge between nations,
   and arbitrate for many peoples.
They will beat their swords into plowshares,
   and their spears into pruning knives.
Nation will not take up sword against nation,
   and they will no longer train for war.

                         (Isa. 2:2–4, AT)

Unlike Cain, and unlike those portrayed in Psalm 10 and in the latter part of Isaiah 2, the nations find their well-being in drawing closer to their Creator. The prophet does not envision this hope for the extremely near future, nor for somewhere outside of human history. It may not come soon, but it is a this-worldly hope.

Now the relationship between arrogance and idolatry in Isaiah 2 can begin to make sense. In verses 7–8 the litter of "stuff" of silver, gold, weaponry—idols, in short—is what humans end up seeking when they neglect the greater project of being what they were made to be. Such inert objects cannot offer security. They not only divert, but drain, and ultimately disappoint and destroy. In contrast, moving toward God, learning from God's ways, as the nations do who seek peace, leads humans to a changed relationship with the objects they fashion. These objects are then not masters, but tools for serving and preserving the earth.

The contrast in Isaiah 2 is not between serving God and ourselves, but rather between serving God and serving idols. The question is not *whether* we will serve, but *whom* and *what* we will serve. We may serve God by tending healthy relationships to one another and to the earth, or we are left serving objects that give us nothing and leave us empty. There are, the Bible repeatedly says, no third options.

Consumerism's Demands

The sad picture of a land littered with silver, gold, and chariots may remind us of our own landscape of "stuff." With half the U.S. national budget going to military spending, we may well wonder whether weaponry has brought security. But military spending is only part of the American search for fulfillment from what money can buy. Nearly everyone in Western society has spent a lifetime surrounded by a consumer culture so pervasive that it is difficult to imagine its absence. A friend of mine tells of her daughter, a high school student, who after growing up in privilege spent a summer among the poor in Kenya. She returned with an altered view of the materialism she had taken for granted before, and proceeded to give away many of her possessions. She realized at an early age what the prophet said long ago: that what we own owns us. If in our travels or our imaginations we have glimpsed other possibilities, we may likewise question our assigned role as consumers.

I remember hearing as a child the drone of radio stock market reports. Phrases like "Dow Jones Industrial Average" glued themselves to my aural memory, along with assurances that the lunch menu included Salisbury steak, mashed potatoes, carrots and peas, rolls, and orange Jello. The voice telling us what was "up five percent" and "down two and a half percent" seemed designed to warn children of the tedious life awaiting us as adults.

Today's stock market reports are jazzier. They include daily attributions of cause and effect and, more strangely, of emotional rollercoasters felt by the stock market. It is not just that stock owners receive the report with joy or nerves—the market itself is anthropomorphized as jittery, elated, depressed, or ebullient. Further, a happy market is a happy public: Americans are psychoanalyzed through the "consumer confidence index," a monthly gauge of optimism about employment and income, an index used to predict the future of retail sales. It assumes that consumers who expect to make more money will spend it. To feel good is to buy goods. We are so often called "confident" when we are poised to shop that we may get confused, thinking family contentment, and even self-esteem, are being measured.

The consumer confidence index evidently does measure spending patterns with some accuracy. But as anyone knows who has ever used shopping as a placebo for boredom or depression, there is something perverse in this "confidence" language. If we really felt confident, would we show it by spending money, or perhaps by singing, or tackling a difficult problem, or writing a check to help vaccinate desperately poor children? And what does it mean if our spending is regulated not by what is needed to feed, clothe, and shelter our families, but by how much money we have (or worse, expect to have)? If shopping is linked with confidence and failure to shop with its lack, what happens to our self-image as citizens, as humans, and as worshipers of God?

As Saint Augustine said, "You have made us for yourself, O Lord, and our heart is restless until it rests in you."[5] Dependence on other gods, or goods, is not a measure of confidence, but of restlessness, a fruitless search for satisfaction elsewhere than in God. The need for God and the need for goods do not really operate on two separate planes, one on Sunday and the other the rest of the week. Rather, they intersect at a vital place within us. Saint Augustine's spiritual restlessness manifests itself in addictions to shopping malls, shopping carts, shopping bags, and shopping days till Christmas. As psychologist Richard Ryan put it, echoing Augustine, "We keep looking outside ourselves for satisfactions that can only come from within."[6]

No generation before ours has been so intensely beset by commercialism. It is more difficult to imagine a world free of billboards, Internet ads, flyers, jingles, and corporate sponsorships of programs, arenas, and even school buses, than it is to imagine nations turning weapons into farm implements: while we know we oppose violence (especially that of others), and while war's ravages are clear, we may not see the damage done by material greed—damage to our own and our family's well-being, to our society, and to the natural world. It is helpful to examine our assumptions about the good life. What is it, and how free are we to live it?

Choices and Happiness

The personal has been progressively removed from buying and selling. Small shops where one could step in from the sidewalk and greet the shopkeeper by name have been replaced by malls on the edge of town; big box stores growing in square footage with each decade; "Anywhere USA" districts of national brand stores, restaurants, coffee shops, and super-supermarkets, surrounded by square miles of parking lot; and finally the virtual megastore on every computer and phone, delivered to our door in a cardboard box. We need not even pause to enter credit card information, much less speak to anyone. With a few keystrokes we can see, want, click, and receive. We need not wonder where the merchandise came from, who made it and at what cost, who will observe our cravings and acquisitions, and in whose neighborhood our stuff will spend eternity once we discard it.

Amazingly, however, the ten thousand choices on offer for the simplest things—breakfast cereal, for instance—do not give more freedom, but overwhelm and paralyze the senses.[7] Such wealth of opportunity has not made us happier. Between the 1950s and the 1990s, Americans more than doubled the number of cars we owned and the miles we drove, used twenty-one times as much plastic, and traveled twenty-five times farther in planes. The size of our homes has much more than doubled. Yet according to the University of Chicago's National Opinion Research Council, the number of Americans who reported being "very happy" reached its peak in the late 1950s, and has been sliding downward ever since.[8] Purchasing power for necessities improves life. But beyond this level, like too much sugar, more purchases leave many feeling worse. Obsolescence becomes instantaneous: once a purchase is made, the thrill is gone, and can only be renewed by finding another want to satisfy.[9] Though Americans have become on average increasingly wealthy, polls consistently show down-ward slides in life satisfaction.[10] And despite superior wealth, we rank below ten other countries in happiness.[11] According to another leading measure of sustainable well-being, the United States ranks sixteenth in experienced well-being and thirty-third in life expectancy, despite having an ecological footprint larger than nearly all the other countries in the world.[12] Clearly we can-not consume our way to happiness.

There are two stories that give pause here. The first is how we arrived here. The second is what consumerism is doing to us.

How We Got Here

My father tells of his siblings' excitement during the Depression when his parents brought home a single tube of toothpaste. Those of us who read *Little Women* or *Little House in the Big Woods* may recall delightful Christmases constructed from a few Bibles or a homemade doll.

Not that all our ancestors lived like the Ingallses or the Alcotts. In 1899, Thorstein Veblen examined critically, and often wryly, the stratum of society given to what he called "conspicuous con-sumption," that is, the open use of what money could buy to assert one's importance and position. As far as he could tell, the purpose of money among society's leisure class was not to meet needs, but to buy status:

> In any community where goods are held in severalty it is necessary . . . that an individual should possess as large a portion of goods as others with whom he is accustomed to class himself; and it is extremely gratifying to possess some-thing more than others. But as fast as a person makes new acquisitions, and becomes accustomed to the resulting new standard of wealth, the new standard forthwith ceases to afford appreciably greater satisfaction than the earlier stan-dard did. The tendency in any case is constantly to make the present pecuniary standard the point of departure for a fresh increase of wealth.[13]

In other words, when luxuries supply self-image, the answer to the question, "How much is enough?" is inevitably "just a little more." In contrast with these few, most of the American public at the time valued thrift. By the late 1920s it was becoming clear to manufacturers that the increasing productivity of their factories was outstripping a frugal public's inclination to buy.[14] In order for the leisure class's wealth to increase, ordinary citizens had to be taught to want more goods. Workers and unions favored rebalancing overproduction by reducing the work week. But many business owners, perceiving that shorter work weeks would erode profits, called thrift a "buyer's strike." They rolled out guilt-seeking slogans such as "Your Purchases Keep America Employed." (Such slogans sound strangely familiar today, as consumer spending is constantly linked to the monthly jobs report.) In 1927, industrial relations counselor E. S. Cowdrick called for "the new economic gospel of consumption," not because the American public was demanding it, but because it was not. In 1929, President Herbert Hoover's Committee on Recent Economic Changes reported that because "wants are almost insatiable" and "one want satisfied makes room for another," therefore, "economically we have a boundless field before us," to be exploited by what the committee called "carefully predeveloped consumption."[15] With those ends in mind, the modern advertising industry was born.

In other words, before the 1920s the American economy grew through increased production. But by the 1920s its growth began to depend on creating consumer demand. It has done so ever since. Despite the questioning in the 1960s, past the oil crisis of the 1970s, and into and beyond the Reagan era, consumerism has come to be taken for granted in America, and increasingly elsewhere. During World War II Americans practiced thrift and self-denial. During the Iraq war, as debts piled higher, we were encouraged to shop. During the economic crisis of the early twenty-first century, when so many overextended families went bankrupt or lost their homes, it became briefly clear that spending without saving had created misery. Yet the drumbeat of economic stimulus continued: families on the edge of disaster were once again encouraged, as a sign of their hope and patriotism, to go out and shop, as if bankrupting themselves would secure economic prosperity and freedom.

What Consumerism Is Doing

Cultural observers note the consumer overload, the "Affluenza" afflicting many—appearing as stress-related symptoms such as headaches, hyperacidity, heart palpitations, depression, anxiety, sleeplessness, irritability—all harking back to a lack of "margins" in the American lifestyle.[16] Many lack space for rest and reflection and suffer from "possession overload," from having too many objects to pay for, care for, and find space for, and too little time or room for family and friends. The rate of clinical depression in the United States is ten times what it was before 1945. "By contrast, Old Order Amish, who avoid most of the amenities of our society, suffer depression less than a fifth as often."[17]

To be sure, religious communities resist consumerism more successfully. The Mennonite writer Doris Janzen Longare's little book *Living More with Less* has been revised, and is filled with suggestions for lives full of people and human values rather than possessions.[18] Duane Elgin's classic *Voluntary Simplicity* draws deeply from religious traditions both Western and Eastern.[19] John F. Kavanaugh, author of *Following Christ in a Consumer Society*, writes as a Jesuit priest.[20] Even those who write on this topic from a secular perspective emphasize valuing people and other parts of creation over the objects humans make. Freedom from the rat race of consumerism serves the public good: "Citizenship requires a commitment of time and attention, a commitment people cannot make if they are lost to themselves in an ever-accelerating cycle of work and consumption."[21]

The economy is usually measured by the Gross Domestic Product (GDP). But many have pointed out what a poor measure of well-being this is, since it rises with increasing health care premiums, military expenditures, and disaster cleanup costs—which all reflect instability and misery rather than prosperity. Several states have adopted other measures. Maryland, for instance, uses the Genuine Progress Indicator, which includes not simply economic but also social and quality-of-life variables such as leisure time, ecological health, and safety.[22]

Consumerism is not just a danger to middle-class well-being and a rival to higher values. As its proceeds have enriched the already wealthy, income gaps have widened. Greed has a way of cloaking itself in contempt, of saying, "I worked hard and earned this; it's nobody's business but my own," that is to say, "God will not seek it out" (Ps. 10:4). Yet the poor watch the same TV commercials as the wealthy, and feel pressure to buy name-brand items they cannot afford, and to finance these purchases through consumer credit that can cost meals, health, and homes. Such pressure is increasingly exerted on the very young. When psychologically sophisticated advertising convinces children to measure their worth by possessions, it's difficult for them to understand why they should suffer deprivation while their TV "friends"— beautiful models and actors—live glamorous, thoughtless lives.

Still more insults await the poor. Factories creating luxury goods are positioned among the world's poorest, often emitting toxins into their air. Working conditions in these factories are often dire and dangerous. And it's not only factories and their waste that end up next to the poor, but also landfills where discarded possessions lie. Western disposable items exported for profit to developing countries lacking in recycling or even trash collection become mountains of diapers and rivers of plastic bottles.

What consumerism does to the natural world is yet another story. Writer Annie Leonard began studying the cycles of consumerism during college, when she noticed the piles of trash awaiting pickup on the streets of New York City. She followed the trash to the Fresh Kills Landfill on Staten Island, whose peaks were eighty feet taller than the Statue of Liberty.[23] The waste she saw there inspired her to research the life cycle of complex products as they are mined, manufactured, transported, consumed, and discarded. She found that at every step in this process, from the extraction of raw resources to the production of goods, from their distribution to their consumption and final disposal, the ecological waste was far greater than we may think. Yet most people have learned to take such practices for granted, presuming that the ecosystem contains infinite capacity to heal itself from all we throw at it.

Finding the Road Less Traveled

The problems with consumer culture are much less frequently heard than the marginal merits of one breakfast cereal or one luxury car over another. If we know less than we ought about the consequences of our lifestyle for the natural world, our neighbors, and ourselves, we need not feel guilty. But once we become aware that slavery to consumption is neither normal nor healthy, once we realize that it is largely the result of others' calculated greed, once we glimpse ourselves not as slaves to human idols but as citizens of communities and responsible, productive, creative adults, we are freer to make choices about what, or whom, we will serve. We are freer to let go of materialism and to cultivate constructive alternatives. Once we recognize the disconnect between shopping and contentment, once we learn reluctance to buy what we will only discard, we can mindfully choose a new relationship between ourselves and our belongings. Things will no longer possess us. Rather, the things we choose to own can become tools for our service of God and creation.

Few people worldwide have homes as large and belongings as numerous as Americans'. Except among those who struggle for necessities, surprisingly little relationship exists between goods and happiness. I have met families in the world's poorest nations, in Haiti, Nepal, and India, for instance, whose possessions are meager by American standards, but whose strength is immeasurable, families living in tiny quarters with few of the comforts Americans consider basic, among whom love, kindness, and generosity reign. To say this is not to romanticize poverty, but rather to suggest that there is something we in America can learn from how others live, something that our spiritual ancestors knew but that we have mostly lost. Proverbs 30:8–9 sums up material need in this way:

> Remove far from me falsehood and lying;
>   give me neither poverty nor riches;
>   feed me with the food that I need,
> or I shall be full, and deny you,
>   and say, "Who is the LORD?"
> or I shall be poor, and steal,
>   and profane the name of my God.

Voluntary simplicity goes against the stream of our own neighbors, our own families, our own habits. We cannot choose what seems like deprivation. But as we see how much junk is tripping us up, how thoroughly homage to material belongings interferes with abundant life, we will seek a different kind of abundance. Elizabeth Canham, the Benedictine oblate whose words began this chapter, goes on to say, "Our question may be, "How do I share the many resources available to me and cease to be dominated by the obsession for more?"[24] She comments:

> The desire for simplicity leads some of us to value skills nearly lost and to search out natural expressions of creativity. When the rediscovery of these skills emerges . . . from a yearning to express the divine within ourselves, then we learn to live more simply and to pray in a more integrated fashion. Our creativity will become our prayer, born of simple attention to what is around us.[25]

Finding God

Isaiah 2:2–4, discussed above, envisions the nations streaming to God for help turning from destruction to fruitful employment. In Matthew 6:25–34, immediately after framing God and money as opposing deities, Jesus offers sound advice against the anxiety of consumerism: "Look at the birds" whom God feeds, and "consider the lilies of the field" whom God clothes in bright array. Stop being anxious about material needs, but "strive first for the kingdom of God and God's righteousness, and all these things will be given to you as well" (v. 33). Drawing closer to God, we find gratitude, we seek to learn, and we trust that our needs will be provided. We enjoy the adventure of living freer from encumbrance and closer to God, other people, and creation.

In the past four chapters we have examined several pervasive contemporary assumptions: the assumption that our present lifestyle is here to stay and need not be reexamined; the assumption that humans may dominate creation with impunity and need not live within limits imposed by the earth's resources; and the assumption that consumerism is the happiest and most fulfilling lifestyle possible. We have also outlined alternative visions. We have glimpsed the adventure of adapting to changing realities. We have heard the invitation to enter humans' rightful place in the larger created world. And we have seen that abundance is available elsewhere than commercial culture. Next we will examine particular ecological issues: food and agriculture, toxic waste, and climate change. How we handle these will determine our legacy, the world we bequeath to our children and our children's children.

Questions for Thought and Discussion

1. What is your mental image of pride? Of idolatry? How do you think these operate in our culture?

2. What do you see in the contrast between Isaiah 2:2–4 and the rest of the chapter? What does it mean to use human-made tools in service of God and others?

3. To what extent do you think humans can live independent of service to God or to idols?

4. Consider Saint Augustine's statement that "the heart is restless until it finds its rest in you." What does it mean? How have you experienced it?

5. Have you ever had "buyer's remorse"? What does it feel like? What might it have been like to have passed up that particular purchase?

6. If your house burned down tomorrow, what would you miss or replace?

7. Think of a recent moment when you have felt contented or joyful. What circumstances led to that feeling? Who was involved? What were you doing?
8. If you were challenged to make three steps toward simplifying your material lifestyle, what would you do? What would result?

Try This at Home

Take some inventories. First, make a list of significant recent purchases. For each item, ask: 1) Was this a want or a need? 2) How has it changed my life? 3) How long will this purchase last, and what will I do with it then?

Second, walk around your home, evaluating the living space. Don't forget the garage and storage shed. How much do you use regularly? How many square feet are simply storage? How much does it cost to cool and heat this space?

Third, take a look at the garbage. If there were no city services, where would this garbage go? What might you buy differently if forced to find a harmless destination for your trash? What items could be reused, composted, or recycled?

From these three inventories, make a list of any changes you would like to make. If you have a family, involve them, discussing the differences between needs and wants. Plan a holiday in which you "fast" from consumerism, including shopping and media, and "feast" on simple pleasures such as reading, baking, hiking, bike riding, singing, gardening, or talking. Discuss how you feel at day's end. Notice how you sleep.

You crown the year with your bounty;
    your wagon tracks overflow with richness.
The pastures of the wilderness overflow,
    the hills gird themselves with joy,
the meadows clothe themselves with flocks,
    the valleys deck themselves with grain,
    they shout and sing together for joy.
                            —Psalm 65:11–13

We have lived our lives by the assumption that what was good for us would be good for the world. . . . We have been wrong. We must change our lives so that it will be possible to live by the contrary assumption, that what is good for the world will be good for us. And that requires that we make the effort to know the world and learn what is good for it.
                    —Wendell Berry, *The Long-Legged House*

Chapter 5

Food for Life

What Food Is For

In chapter 4 we discussed commodities that we buy and use, distinguishing needs from artificially induced wants. In the next two chapters we will discuss food, a necessity for all living beings. This chapter concerns crops and chapter 6 concerns animals.

When Moses leads the Israelites into the wilderness in Exodus, they learn to depend on God, who provides manna for forty years. Early on, at Mount Sinai, they also learn rules that will govern the eating and sharing of food in their future homeland. God instructs them to use the earth's bounty for its real purpose—not wealth for a few, but sustenance for all.

Physically, food provides energy and nutrients for life, growth, and health. Socially, food's meaning goes far beyond this and is experienced in very different ways by rich and poor. In many locales food can be found in its natural state and eaten close to where it grows. But in our culture, and increasingly elsewhere, food is commodified, transformed from its natural states into conveniently packaged and not necessarily healthful versions, transported far and sold under brand names whose ownership is consolidated into fewer and fewer corporations. Whereas households were once net producers, we have increasingly become consumers in a wasteful system.

73

This consolidated anonymity has created several new problems. The world's food production has increased and there is now, theoretically, enough for everyone. Yet food insecurity continues to haunt the poor here and abroad. In many places, land that was once distributed for subsistence farming has been consolidated for cash crops, leaving many landless and dependent on buying imported food at high and variable prices. Many communities even in the United States, both urban and rural, have become "food deserts," lacking realistic access to nutritious food. Those without personal transportation are forced to depend on sodium-rich, fat-rich, carbohydrate-rich—but nutrient-poor—processed foods that can be obtained from nearby convenience stores and fast food restaurants. The health results are devastating, as this report from Louisville, Kentucky, shows:

> In West Louisville, an area considered one of Louisville's "food deserts," 37% of residents report having high blood pressure, 74% report being overweight or obese, and 12% report having diabetes. Lifestyle and behavioral risk factors cannot explain these statistics alone. In most cases, the choices we make are shaped by the choices we have.[1]

The report cites a study in the *American Journal of Public Health* showing fruit and vegetable intake increasing by 32 percent for each additional grocery store nearby.[2]

In addition to malnutrition, wide distribution of consolidated foods has made food-borne illnesses more difficult to trace and outbreaks more widespread, killing five thousand Americans and costing $152 billion each year. For example, in July 2010 the Centers for Disease Control and Prevention detected a spike in salmonella poisoning nationwide.[3] It was eventually traced to two farms in Iowa, where massive contamination had gone undetected. Inspection disclosed manure piled eight feet high, chickens walking through manure to egg-laying areas, liquid manure streaming through gaps in containment, live rodents and wild birds in the henhouses, and a host of other problems. Eggs from these farms had been distributed under forty-seven labels.

Because we spend money daily on eating and drinking, food and water are prime targets for mass commodification. We will begin with a surprising example, and then explore some of what the Bible says about food practices, examining biblical bottom lines for food production, consumption, and sharing.

Commodified Water

Many Americans have learned to ignore the well-regulated liquid flowing from faucets and fountains around us, and instead purchase water in plastic bottles for approximately twice what gasoline has ever cost, gallon for gallon. Bottled water's popularity shows just how far commodification has gone. It is as powerful a tribute to advertising as we may imagine.

A recent water bill shows that each gallon our family used cost .88 cents, less than a penny. One penny buys nine pint glasses, about the same as nine half-liter bottles. If I buy one bottle for 89 cents instead, I am paying approximately 800 times, or 80,000 percent of, what I would pay by filling up my reusable bottle or glass at the tap. Citizens block even one-percent tax increases, yet willingly increase their water expense every day by *eighty thousand times* that. They do this to buy water that is less regulated than public water—in fact, 40 percent of bottled water *is* tap water, though from a different location.[4] We drink this not just in the Sonoran Desert, but within steps of multiple faucets.

Most plastic bottles are not recycled. Many spend eternity in fields, rivers, streams, and oceans. Some go to landfills. Even when manufacturers change to 30 percent plant material and 100 percent recyclable, what costs money is also ecologically costly.

This orgy of waste suggests that consumer spending, even on basic needs, is not necessarily informed or rational, but is often based on impulse, emotion, misinformation, fashion, image, and perceived convenience. Every few hours we make important choices affecting not only our own health but the health of others and of the planet. Every time we eat or drink, we cast a vote for the nourishment we wish to see available.

Manna

In Exodus, God freed the Israelites from Egypt, a land where they had been forced to build food storage cities for a power-hungry king. This pharaoh was so hard-hearted that when Moses requested a holiday for the slaves, the king preferred to bring all Egypt to ruin through plague after plague (5:1–2; 8:1–32). So extreme was the slaves' misery that Moses called Egypt an "iron-smelting furnace" (Deut. 4:20).

The cruelty of such ancient rulers extended not just to foreigners, but also to their own subjects. Scripture tells of a highly stratified society in which, to avoid starvation, Egyptians were forced to sell themselves and their land to the king (Gen. 47:19). Archaeology supports this view as well. Numerous figurines and drawings found in Egyptian royal tombs depict spinners, weavers, farmers, and fishers laboring under watchful supervision, their toil enriching their rulers.[5] As Ellen Davis explains, "The wealth of the land flowed upward, away from the small farmers, serfs, and slaves who composed the overwhelming majority of the population, to the large landowners, the nobility, the great temples, and the crown."[6]

The economic system instituted by God in the wilderness could hardly contrast more. The first two events after the Israelites cross the sea illustrate this new reality. Two crises occur—a shortage of water, and then a food shortage.

In the first case, the water is too bitter to drink. God directs Moses to throw a piece of wood into it, and it becomes drinkable (Exod. 15:23–25). Soon the Israelites reach an oasis with twelve springs (v. 27). One of these events suffices; both together show extravagant grace. By this, God shows what ruling well means: not domination and extraction but provision and care.

In the second crisis, when the people complain of hunger, God tells Moses, "'I am going to rain bread from heaven for you, and each day the people shall go out and gather enough for that day. In that way I will test them, whether they will follow my instruction or not. On the sixth day, when they prepare what they bring in, it will be twice as much as they gather on other days'" (Exod. 16:4–5).

This is the manna's story:

In the morning there was a layer of dew around the camp. When the layer of dew lifted, there on the surface of the wilderness was a fine flaky substance, as fine as frost on the ground. When the Israelites saw it, they said to one another, "What is it?" For they did not know what it was. Moses said to them, "It is the bread that the LORD has given you to eat. This is what the LORD has commanded: 'Gather as much of it as each of you needs, an omer to a person according to the number of persons, all providing for those in their own tents.'" The Israelites did so, some gathering more, some less. But when they measured it with an omer, those who gathered much had nothing over, and those who gathered little had no shortage; they gathered as much as each of them needed. And Moses said to them, "Let no one leave any of it over until morning." But they did not listen to Moses; some left part of it until morning, and it bred worms and became foul. And Moses was angry with them. Morning by morning they gathered it, as much as each needed; but when the sun grew hot, it melted.

On the sixth day they gathered twice as much food, two omers apiece. When all the leaders of the congregation came and told Moses, he said to them, "This is what the LORD has commanded: 'Tomorrow is a day of solemn rest, a holy sabbath to the LORD; bake what you want to bake and boil what you want to boil, and all that is left over put aside to be kept until morning.'" So they put it aside until morning, as Moses commanded them; and it did not become foul, and there were no worms in it. Moses said, "Eat it today, for today is a sabbath to the LORD; today you will not find it in the field. Six days you shall gather it; but on the seventh day, which is a sabbath, there will be none." (Exod. 16:13b–26)

This manna sustains the Israelites every day until, forty years later, they begin eating the produce of the promised land (Josh. 5:12).

Though a generous gift from God, the manna comes with some clear principles. First, everyone has enough. Since no one has more than another, circumstances enforce equality. Second, the manna spoils after one day, so they are no more able to hoard it than they can the air they breathe. For people who had spent their lives building storage cities for hoarding, food that cannot be used for economic exploitation is new. They can enjoy their daily bread without thought of economic gain and without worry of loss.[7] Third, the manna keeps Sabbath, allowing its gatherers to do so.

Thus the forty years become a training ground, a period of formation. The manna's peculiar properties seem designed to shape habits, so that a group of choiceless slaves becomes a nation living in dependence on their God and equality with neighbors. Everyone has his or her share, and no one can use the supply limits for profit. The manna does not serve gain or prestige. Rather, it serves nutritional needs, giving energy for life's activities. And the Sabbath rest from gathering is reinforced more than two thousand times, every week for forty years.

Food Rules

Considering that the first break with God and with the earth in Genesis 3 was over food, and considering food's fundamental links to ethics, its prominent place in the wilderness stories should not surprise us. Nor should it surprise us that, when the Israelites arrive at Mount Sinai and receive rules for their life in Canaan, food continues to be high on the agenda.

The constrained behavior of manna imposes physical limits on what the Israelites can do with food. But in the land flowing with milk and honey, food will abound. It is the garden of Eden in reverse: In Genesis 3 God had replaced a moral prohibition with a physical boundary, denying access to the garden. But when the Israelites enter the land, physical constraints on the food supply will vanish. Yet the people must still adhere to moral boundaries, rules governing the land, the planting and harvesting of fields, the food choices, the sharing of food, and the treatment, killing, and eating of animals.

The rules for fields in the land follow the same principles as the manna did. First, just as the manna belongs to God, so acreage in the new land is a loan, and only a loan, from God: "The land shall not be sold in perpetuity, for the land is mine; with me you are but aliens and tenants" (Lev. 25:23). The people aren't free to take it away from one another. The land must ideally stay within families (Lev. 25:25–28), even if economic hardship befalls some members. If it is sold, it reverts to the original owner every half century to narrow the gap between rich and poor (vv. 13–16).

Second, concern for the disadvantaged remains. Food is a basic right for all, including poor and non-Israelite neighbors. Equitable distribution will no longer come miraculously, but through voluntary self-control and generosity: "When you reap the harvest of your land, you shall not reap to the very edges of your field, or gather the gleanings of your harvest. You shall not strip your vineyard bare, or gather the fallen grapes of your vineyard; you shall leave them for the poor and the alien: I am the LORD your God" (Lev. 19:9–10).

Scripture's most famous gleaner illustrates the human potential recovered by such food sharing. To save herself and her mother-in-law from starvation, the Moabite woman Ruth gleans diligently in the fields surrounding Bethlehem (Ruth 2). Her life-saving work eventuates in her marriage to the field's owner and in the birth of the grandfather of King David. Lives are saved, children born, and history made through the rules of shared harvest.

Third, both the manna and the Sinai food rules restrict labor. The Sabbath reappears in the Ten Commandments as a rest for family, employees, and livestock (Exod. 20:8–11). Sabbath rest is also instituted on the scale of years for the sake of the fields themselves, for the poor, and even for the wild animals: "For six years you shall sow your land and gather in its yield; but the seventh year you shall let it rest and lie fallow, so that the poor of your people may eat; and what they leave the wild animals may eat. You shall do the same with your vineyard, and with your olive orchard" (Exod. 23:10–11; see also Lev. 25:1–7). Just as dominion in Genesis 1:26 meant not domination for human enrichment, but taking charge for the benefit of all, so here, stewardship of time means following practices that are generous to the community, kind to animals, and sustainable for the land that supplies all nutrition.

Even though the promised land will provide more variety, Sinai's rules continue to impose dietary limits. Kosher laws list meats forbidden at any time, such as pork, shellfish, and certain game (Lev. 12:1–31). During holy seasons such as Passover, special restrictions apply (Exod. 12:14–22; Deut. 16:1–8). The Day of Atonement requires self-denial and fasting (Lev. 23:27). The discipline of such self-limitations, some perpetual and some seasonal, daily renews awareness of food choices, and reinforces connections between devotion and everyday life. Thus food becomes a channel for reverent gratitude.

Most observant Jews still follow food rules based on these biblical commands, eating only kosher meats, abstaining from certain foods at certain times, and fasting periodically. Observant Muslims similarly abstain from pork and alcohol perpetually, and during Ramadan fast from sunrise to sunset. Such self-discipline encourages other kinds of self-control, such as refraining from anger, gossip, usury, and cheating.

Acts 15 relates the release of Gentile Christians from Jewish law. Christians sometimes see this story as license to disconnect deity and diet. Yet even here Gentile Christians must avoid certain foods (v. 20). Paul likewise clarifies a rationale for abstentions: Christians restrict their eating not from fear or superstition, but from regard for others. "'All things are lawful,'" he quotes, adding, "but not all things are beneficial. 'All things are lawful,' but not all things build up" (1 Cor. 10:23).

Especially since the Reformation, fasting and abstention have been much more loosely held by Christians than by Jews and Muslims. Today Catholics may fast on Ash Wednesday and Good Friday, and abstain from meat on Lenten Fridays. Some Protestants practice voluntary abstentions during Lent. Individuals may choose their own fasts for particular purposes. Despite having fewer programmed restrictions, Christians can use voluntary fasts to practice impulse control, to understand suffering, and to pray more mindfully.

While a great many other ethical principles can be seen in the Sinai laws, the ones outlined above concerning food are plenty to chew on: 1) the land as a sacred trust, farmed to sustain productivity and worker well-being; 2) justice in food distribution; 3) limits on working days and crop production, and on what may be eaten and when.

Contemporary Food Systems

Advertising conveys a natural, happy, nostalgic food production system. Consumers are still invited to county fairs to "come meet Elsie," Borden's smiling cow. The Green Giant grins proudly in the foreground of rolling green fields bursting with vegetables. A lush Hidden Valley basks under blue skies on ranch dressing bottles. A Certified Angus Beef stands in silhouette on an impressionistic hilltop. Swift Pork shows no pig, but a red barn and silo and a prominent ear of corn. Perdue features a quaint farmhouse with a chicken coop nestled beside it, surrounded by trees, sunshine, and space. Such images resemble children's picture books, sentimental and soothing.

Consumers must inquire past the labels to learn how food production actually works. We may think the food industry's mission is to feed populations healthy and reasonably priced foods while maintaining land fertility and returning a just wage to its workers. Given the enormous investments in research and technology over the past century, farming should be healthier and more profitable than ever before.

Agronomists, economists, veterinarians, farmers, and nutritionists are pointing out, however, that our dominant food system is not working well. Much of the fare being produced and sold throughout the United States and overseas is less than healthy, sustainable, and supportive of farmers. There are many complex reasons, some of which we will explore in depth, but the overarching theme is that what was once "agri-culture," that is, the cultivation of the earth and its living resources, has become "agribusiness." Farms once maintained ecological balance out of local necessity. Now the dominant model resembles a factory in which "inputs" are bought and "outputs" are sold or wasted. Often the companies supplying the inputs also buy the outputs, profiting on both ends. Four corporations control 80 percent of American beef, and two control three-fourths of global grain. Nearly 90 percent of American chicken is grown for large companies that control broiler houses holding 30,000 birds each.[8]

Concerns have increasingly been raised over a food system characterized by the opposite of biblical standards: land degradation, food and land centralization, economic injustice, unconcern for ecological limitations, and thoughtless animal cruelty. Thousands of years of development should have brought norms at least as ethical as those of the biblical writers, particularly since scientific and technological advances have facilitated more choices. Yet we rarely see them. These two chapters cannot cover all important food issues, but I will discuss some key concerns and name others.

Land and Field Use

In *The Omnivore's Dilemma*, Michael Pollan describes his visit to a farm in Iowa owned by one family since 1919.[9] Two generations before, not only corn but other vegetables, fruits, and grains grew there, as well as pigs, cattle, chickens, and horses. Animals ate inexpensively from pasture grass and vegetation that humans could not eat, and pastures and gardens were fertilized inexpensively from animal manure: a relatively closed ecological system low in both waste and want.[10] Such a farm would provide most of the family's own food and extra to sell. But today, this Iowa farm produces only corn and soybeans. Though productive, it stays solvent with difficulty. As Pollan puts it, contemporary practice takes the elegant solution of the small farm and neatly divides it into two new problems: "a fertility problem on the farm (which must be remedied with chemical fertilizers) and a pollution problem on the feedlot,"[11] often separated from each other by hundreds of miles.

Pollan outlines the history of American corn production. Depression-era New Deal legislation had attempted to stabilize the price of corn by storing it during times of surplus, assuring farmers a steadier income. Since that time, and especially since the 1970s, farm policy has increasingly favored much larger farms,[12] "agribusinessmen," and buyers such as Cargill—the largest privately held corporation in the world—and Archer Daniels Midland. These two corporations together buy a third of all American corn.[13] Rather than storing surplus grain to sell gradually, the government began subsidizing it directly, encouraging ever more surplus and driving down farmers' incomes while increasing their productivity. In such a system, farmers pour more chemical fertilizers into more land to produce more bushels of corn that net less profit.

Taxpayer-supported subsidies comprise a significant percentage of farm income. But the benefits go primarily to corporations. When production is high and prices fall, corporate conglomerates buy more corn for less. When prices rise, the farmers' cost in seed corn and other inputs rises, enriching the same companies. Though the gross profit from each bushel of grain may increase, farmers can actually net less.[14] In addition, Wall Street speculators in commodities futures, who neither sow nor reap nor ever see or touch this grain, drive and benefit from price fluctuations.[15] Meanwhile, 93 percent of farmers in 2005, up from 27 percent in 1945, supplemented their income with off-farm jobs that typically paid much more than farming did.[16] This trend continues even as commodity prices increase: in 2009, small and mid-sized farms, averaging 1,100 acres in size, yielded net incomes of less than $20,000.[17] When increased demand for corn ethanol drove corn prices skyward, excited farmers planted even more acres of corn, only to see them swept away in drought.

As American corn production has risen from 4 billion bushels in 1970 to 10 billion today, it has found complex outlets, barely recognizable as "daily bread." When grain prices were low, corn was increasingly exported to flood foreign markets, ruining indigenous farmers, leaving whole nations vulnerable when prices rose. Recent competition from ethanol demand, based on government-mandated biofuel targets, has dramatically raised corn's price, contributing to food insecurity in poorer nations.[18] Corn ethanol not only competes with hungry people but also soaks up nearly as much fossil fuel in production as it displaces in the gas tank.[19]

Corn is also used to feed livestock, primarily in concentrated animal feeding operations, producing one pound of beef for every ten pounds of grain.[20] Along with soybeans, corn is the ubiquitous ingredient in processed foods, not only as cereal, grits, and corn meal, but also as additives such as high fructose corn syrup, which sweetens soft drinks, contributing to obesity. Thus, rather than sustaining life and health as they were meant to do, corn and other commodity grains paradoxically create two ills: hunger abroad and obesity at home.[21]

The earth can grow enough food for everyone, but not when it is wasted in these ways. Corporations such as Cargill and Archer Daniels Midland profit across the system, providing pesticides and fertilizers, operating grain elevators and slaughterhouses, brokering and shipping exports, milling corn, feeding livestock, distilling ethanol, manufacturing high-fructose corn syrup and other corn-based processed food ingredients, and helping write the agricultural policies governing these enterprises.

If a few large corporations profit from this system, its losers extend from the land that is degraded by intensive farming, to rivers and streams and their watery inhabitants that are killed by fertilizer runoff, to consumers buying foods contributing to obesity and other health problems, to the insured who help bear obesity-related healthcare costs,[22] to the poor who cannot afford ever-increasing grocery prices, and to taxpayers who support not only government subsidies, but also financial bailouts for commodity market speculators, military operations for foreign petroleum (15 percent used in industrial agriculture),[23] and cleanup of oil spills and ground and water pollution.[24]

For farmers, employees, and eaters who hold a stake in the American food system, the questions being raised can be threatening, and the prospect of change upsetting. But we must ask how well this system is working, and what the alternatives might be.

Travel-Weary Foods

When one drives the countryside of the southern Midwest, fencerow-to-fencerow corn and soybean production is inescapable. I frequently take students to Israel and Palestine where the landscapes are very different. Throughout the Galilee and along the Jordan River one sees plantations of trees—citrus, banana, date, olive, avocado—and fields of cucumbers, tomatoes, lettuce, onions, and other vegetables.

Similar variety can grow here. In the southern Midwest, for example, the agricultural year begins in March with broccoli, asparagus, and greens, and extends to November, December, or beyond. From April on, farmers' markets overflow with goods. Yet throughout these plenteous summers and falls, most of our fields are filled with commodity grains, and grocery stores are stockpiled with produce that travels farther than many of us do, farther than most of our grandparents ever did, let alone their meals. Why is most food, even in fertile regions, trucked or flown in from afar? And what is this system costing?

Consider the tomato. I usually begin seeds indoors. Once, when I enriched the soil with compost made by red wriggler worms, what grew were not the seeds I planted, but tomato seeds from the compost. These unplanned-for seedlings were hardly necessary, because half the tomatoes we grew that year sprouted as volunteers, children of the previous year's garden. Had the harvest been insufficient, we had simply to walk to the farmers' market where a variety of mottled and striped heirlooms were being sampled and sold. The tomato has a will to live, thrive, diversify, and propagate—as do many other foods.

Yet throughout the local growing season, grocery superstores import round, red, lookalike tomatoes flown from the south.[25] "Strip-mined in Texas," as storyteller Garrison Keillor once described them, more delightful in a still-life painting than on one's tongue. Travel can be broadening for humans, but it simply makes vegetables old. International shipment has enabled us to eat, year round, every food we desire—or at least a replica of it, picked green and ripened in transport. Yet each Peruvian grape and each Mexican lettuce leaf consumes more calories in fuel than it brings us to eat.

Some call this "eating fossil fuels." Thirty-nine percent of fruits, 12 percent of vegetables, 40 percent of lamb, and 78 percent of fish eaten in the United States are internationally imported, atrophying local infrastructures. "As fossil fuels become less abundant and more expensive, this system will become increasingly strained until it finally collapses, leaving local communities without the ability to feed themselves."[26] Without local farms we would live at the mercy of the centralized food distribution of a few pharaohs.

Gary Paul Nabhan, director of the Center for Sustainable Environments at Northern Arizona University, spent a year eating what grew within two hundred miles of Flagstaff, Arizona. He discovered that even the desert yielded abundance.[27] His experiment has been replicated over and over in other parts of the country.[28] Every year, farmers' markets are expanding their offerings of fruits, vegetables, meats, and homemade breads, soups, cheeses, salsas, soaps, and even tamales. Independently owned grocery stores increasingly feature local products. The growth of these markets depends on buyer response. Every time we eat, we vote on, and invest ourselves in, the system we prefer.

At home we often take a grateful tour of the dinner table: "Bread and eggs came from the Millers; Kenny made the cheese; David and Gail grew the lettuce. The Lewises gave us the apples, and everything else came from the garden." This litany reflects not only the anticipation of wholesome freshness, but the joy of friendship and the satisfaction of growing our garden and helping nearby farmers. This intimately local movement is growing worldwide. Our conservation biologist relatives in Nepal work with indigenous farmers to preserve seed diversity and develop grains appropriate for Nepali soil and markets, resisting globalization.[29]

"Locavores" offer many personal reasons for their diets. Some choose to eat locally because fresh foods taste good and contribute to health. Others wish to support local economies and sustainable farms or to eliminate packaging and needless food transport. Some want to demonstrate their seriousness to policymakers. Others enjoy the spiritual discipline of fasting from foods out of season and celebrating each species in its time. Some say it is easier to pray their gratitude for farmers whose names are known. Others relish the self-sufficiency of a meal grown outside corporate channels. For some people of faith it simply seems right to resist a pharaoh-like system in which food serves to increase wealth for only a few, and to choose a system more closely resembling biblical norms, in which food is made for eating, for sharing, for pleasure, and for the health of both humans and land.

Pharaoh's System Replicated in Judah

Ancient Israelites escaped the pharaoh only to institute a home-grown fiefdom. During King Solomon's reign, his dining hall required daily inputs of "thirty cors of choice flour, and sixty cors of meal, ten fat oxen, and twenty pasture-fed cattle, one hundred sheep, besides deer, gazelles, roebucks, and fatted fowl" (1 Kgs. 4:22–23), as well as barley and straw for forty thousand royal horses, and annual donations of wheat and oil for his benefactor and lumber supplier, King Hiram of Tyre (5:11).[30] Each sentence becomes more surprising than the last: "Solomon also had seventy thousand laborers and eighty thousand stonecutters in the hill country, besides Solomon's three thousand three hundred supervisors who were over the work" (5:15–16)—that is, the work of building Solomon's temple. This happened, the narrator says with no detectable irony, "in the four hundred eightieth year after the Israelites came out of the land of Egypt" (6:1). The pharaoh's system became Israel's own, justified by religious piety. But building did not stop with the temple. It continued to Solomon's own palace, "all of Solomon's storage cities, the cities for his chariots, the cities for his cavalry, and whatever Solomon desired to build, in Jerusalem, in Lebanon, and in all the land of his dominion" (9:19). Having escaped the pharaoh's food economy, the Israelites bred rulers who recreated it for their own profit.

This imperial system broke the nation when, after Solomon's death, most of the tribes seceded, refusing to participate in homemade slavery. Such a devastating history should warn us against enthralling ourselves to new fiefdoms.

Biologically speaking, there is only one way that humans and other animals obtain food. Whether we forage fruits and hunt game, or whether we farm, whether we eat plants directly or indirectly through eating animals, whether we grow and cook our own food or eat TV dinners from the supermarket, we feed ourselves from the earth. At the same time, as the two contrasting systems illustrate—the slave economy of empires and the divine economy of Mount Sinai—fundamentally different food cultures may exist side by side, both in the ancient world and in ours.

In Sinai's economy, food's purpose is energy for life's activities. It is a basic right for all. It is not designed to enrich anyone at the expense of other people, or animals, or the land itself. It does not extract from land, laborers, or buyers without returning the means to sustain.

In the royal system, whether that of foreign pharaohs or that of domestic lords, food is a commodity designed to enrich the few. It may be extracted from low-paying labor. It may exploit citizens and foreigners. It may be harvested without heed to ecological cost. In this system, sellers must keep buyers from understanding the sources and means of production. They must keep the consumer eye trained on convenience, packaging, coupons, and bargains. These paradigms have been called "two nearly opposite ways of understanding ourselves, our fellow creatures, and our world."[31]

Certainly not all actual projects fall neatly under one paradigm or the other. But distinctions in governing principles are clear, and distinctions in practice may be ferreted out. Though more consumers are becoming aware of their choices, we have a vast distance yet to go. People of faith who recognize the purpose of food in a just society can help others to better understand what is happening, how it affects our communities, and how we may promote health for growers, eaters, and land.

Questions for Thought and Discussion

1. Reflect on your family's own rituals and attitudes toward food. In what ways are meals celebrated with gratitude

toward growers and producers, toward animals and plants, toward God?

2. What purposes do you think underlie Scripture's food rules? How do they compare to the uses of food in contemporary culture?

3. What kind of living do you think farmers should make from their labor and skill? What are helpful uses of cropland and what practices do you question?

4. If land ultimately belongs to its Creator, what role do humans play in its care? How can those of us who do not own land contribute to its welfare?

5. What daily "food rules" do you follow or want to follow? What do you see practiced in your church and community?

Try This at Home

Buy each family member a permanent water bottle to refill at taps and water fountains.

Take inventory of your pantry and refrigerator and notice where your foods originated. Read ingredient labels. Can you pronounce the chemical names, and do you know what they are? Look them up on the Internet. (Michael Pollan wryly suggests avoiding what our great-grandmothers would not recognize and what third graders can't pronounce.[32])

Plan a local harvest meal. Visit the nearest farmers' market and plan your meal around what you find. Ask farmers how to prepare that unusual squash. Give yourself extra credit for trash reduction.

If you have children, research your local agricultural year together. What grows when? Make a date to visit a nearby U-Pick farm together, and produce a pie or meal from what you bring home. Try freezing or canning what you can't use right away.

Try growing something you haven't grown before in your yard, on the balcony, or in a community garden. Experiment with something easy, like tomatoes or lettuce, and don't worry about failures. Enjoy the process.

The righteous care for the needs of their animals,
but the kindest acts of the wicked are cruel.
—Proverbs 12:10, NIV

In the modern West, animal husbandry has largely been
replaced by systematized brutality and exploitation quite
unlike good farming practice in the past and in a different
league of evil even from bad farming practice in the past. It
cannot possibly be justified by reference to the Bible. Cru-
cially, the Bible does not regard domestic animals as mere
objects for people to use, but, like wild animals, as subjects
of their own lives.
—Richard Bauckham, *The Bible and Ecology:*
Rediscovering the Community of Creation

Chapter 6

The Needs of Animals

Scripture and Animals

We began our discussion of food in chapter 5 by contrasting two systems: the imperial slavery from which Israelites emerged and the dominion God established in the wilderness. Unlike the pharaoh's system, God's did not enrich a few at the expense of many, but provided health and energy for all. It sustained the land's bounty; provided rest for workers and animals; set aside food for the needy, foreigners, and wild beasts; and regularly rebalanced the gap between rich and poor. It also commended self-limitations, both seasonally and perpetually, on what and how the people eat. This chapter will further explore animal treatment according to Scripture and present practice.

The Sinai commands are positioned as a divine "Plan B," not the ideal but a move toward restoration after humans broke our original bonds with God, the land, and one another. The stories of Eden, Cain, and the flood, describing this alienation, are book-ended by two contrasting comments about animals. In Genesis 1:29–30, God gives only the plants as food for humans and animals alike:

> "See, I have given you every plant yielding seed that is upon the face of all the earth, and every tree with seed in its fruit;

you shall have them for food. And to every beast of the earth, and to every bird of the air, and to everything that creeps on the earth, everything that has the breath of life, I have given every green plant for food."

But after the flood, God says:

"The fear and dread of you shall rest on every animal of the earth, and on every bird of the air, on everything that creeps on the ground, and on all the fish of the sea; into your hand they are delivered. Every moving thing that lives shall be food for you; and just as I gave you the green plants, I give you everything." (Gen. 9:2–3)

Hope nevertheless remains that predation is not our final state:

The wolf shall live with the lamb,
the leopard shall lie down with the kid,
the calf and the lion and the fatling together,
and a little child shall lead them.
The cow and the bear shall graze,
their young shall lie down together;
and the lion shall eat straw like the ox.
The nursing child shall play over the hole of the asp,
and the weaned child shall put its hand on the adder's den.
They will not hurt or destroy
on all my holy mountain;
for the earth will be full of the knowledge of the Lord
as the waters cover the sea.

(Isa. 11:6–9)

Isaiah's vision reminds readers that the present course is less than ideal. If even wild cats can be imagined enjoying their vegetables, we may ponder the choices we omnivores have, what the eating of animals means, and how to eat in ways that honor both Creator and creation.

Even in the world of animal consumption in which Israelites find themselves, where universal vegetarianism is only a wistful story of creation's younger days and a wish for its ultimate goal, the Sinai commands impose severe limits concerning the animals Israelites may eat (Lev. 11:1–30).[1] According to Leviticus, far more animals may not be eaten than may.[2] Even these must be slaughtered humanely. Their blood cannot be consumed, but is either given to God on the altar or buried (Lev. 17:10–14) "as acknowledgment that bringing death to living things is a concession of God's grace and not a privilege of [human] whim."[3]

Leviticus 1–7 details various prescribed sacrifices. Not all of these are sin offerings; some, like those of Cain and Abel, express thanks. Nor do all offerings consist of meat. Grain, oil, wine, fruits, and vegetables are also given. Some offerings go wholly to God, or to God and the priests. One, the "sacrifice of well-being," is eaten by the whole family. In fact, according to Leviticus 17:3–4, the only way to eat meat is sacramentally:

> If anyone of the house of Israel slaughters an ox or a lamb or a goat in the camp, or slaughters it outside the camp, and does not bring it to the entrance of the tent of meeting, to present it as an offering to the LORD before the tabernacle of the LORD, he shall be held guilty of bloodshed; he has shed blood, and he shall be cut off from the people.

According to this tradition, without thanksgiving slaughter is simply bloodshed. Though nonviolent provision had long since gone the way of Eden, animal lives were taken sparingly, and always in their Creator's presence.[4] The point for us is not to return to these practices, nor even to view them as the best ones traditional culture offers. But their reverence for life is worth comparing to today's practices.

The traditional assumptions not only of our spiritual ancestors but of the land on which Americans live challenge us to consider what we do. Eating practices of many Native American tribes demonstrate respect for animals. Theologian George Tinker, whose own heritage is Osage and Cherokee, says:

> Animals, birds, crops, and medicines are all living relatives and must be treated with respect if they are to be genuinely efficacious for the people. The ideal of harmony and balance requires that all share a respect for all other existent things, avoiding gratuitous or unthinking acts of violence. Maintaining harmony and balance requires that all necessary acts of violence be done in a sacred way. Thus nothing is taken from the earth without prayer and offering.[5]

If our current habits fall short of those of both our spiritual ancestors and our land, we must ask why, and whether anyone's gain is worth the losses.

Scripture also commends humane treatment of livestock. The fourth commandment enjoins Sabbath rest for animals as well as humans. In fact, its placement of ox, donkey, and all livestock in the middle of a list that begins with "you, your son or your daughter" and concludes with "the resident alien in your towns" (Deut. 5:14; cf. Exod. 20:10) defies the great gulf modern people imagine between ourselves and other creatures. Other provisions likewise concern animal welfare. An ox threshing grain should not be muzzled, but allowed to eat (Deut. 25:4). Israelites are responsible not only for well-being of their own animals but for that of neighbors' animals. Even an enemy's ox or donkey must led home if it wanders, and set free from a burdensome load (Exod. 23:4–5). Two animals of unequal strength may not be yoked together, overworking the weaker one (Deut. 22:10). Israelites were expected, in short, to behave toward animals as their God did, the God who enjoyed animals before humans ever walked the earth (Gen. 1:21–25); who feeds the birds (Matt. 6:26); who boasts over animals' magnificence without concern for their human usefulness (Job 39); who "saves humans and animals alike" (Ps. 36:6); who gives animals their food (146:9) and is praised by wild and domestic beasts, creeping things and flying birds (148:10); whose prophets and sages compare animals favorably to people (Isa. 1:3; Jer. 8:7) and commend learning from them (Prov. 6:6–8; Job 12:7–8).

In 2 Samuel, after King David has made a woman pregnant and then killed her husband to cover up his misdeeds, the prophet Nathan awakens the king's conscience with a tale of two neighbors. The richer man had many flocks and herds, but the poorer man had only one lamb:

> "He brought it up, and it grew up with him and with his children; it used to eat of his meager fare, and drink from his cup, and lie in his bosom, and it was like a daughter to him. Now there came a traveler to the rich man, and he was loath to take one of his own flock or herd to prepare for the wayfarer who had come to him, but he took the poor man's lamb, and prepared that for the guest who had come to him." (2 Sam. 12:3–4)

With these poignant details Nathan teases out the murderous king's compassion. There is no hint that Nathan, David, or the storyteller considered the poor man's attachment sentimental. On the contrary, the king reacts by decreeing that "the man who has done this deserves to die" (v. 5), estimating the act not as theft but murder. In a culture indifferent to human-animal attachments, Nathan's calculated story would fall flat. But instead it arouses outrage in the king and in ancient and modern readers.

If everyone who eats is, as Wendell Berry said, "farming by proxy,"[6] we must ask how even those who do not farm can make choices living up to biblical standards. Are there ways to eat some animals and enjoy others as companions and helpers as our ancestors did, ways that honor God's care for all, maintain our own health and integrity, and protect ecological well-being?

Animals in Christian Interpretation

Christian theology has a mixed record, more mixed than that of Scripture. On the one hand, even the critic Lynn White could find a patron saint for ecologists in St. Francis, saying:

> The key to an understanding of Francis is his belief in the
> virtue of humility—not merely for the individual but for
> man as a species. . . . With him the ant is no longer simply
> a homily for the lazy, flames a sign of the thrust of the soul
> toward union with God; now they are Brother Ant and Sis-
> ter Fire, praising the Creator in their own ways, as Brother
> Man does in his.[7]

Biologist Charles Birch and theologian Lukas Vischer likewise
commend Francis, and point out several other saints, including
Jerome in the fourth century, who said, "Since Christ came at the
end of the ages and restored omega to alpha, taking the end back
to the beginning, we no longer eat meat."[8] Many desert monks
adopted vegetarianism alongside other spiritual disciplines.

Jerome's contemporary Augustine, on the other hand, said
that "the irrational animals that fly, swim, walk, or creep . . . are
dissociated from us by their want of reason, and are therefore
by the just appointment of the Creator subjected to us to kill or
keep alive for our own uses."[9] Thomas Aquinas, writing his comprehensive *Summa Theologica* in the thirteenth century, quoted
Augustine to argue that animals are designed for use by humans,
the more perfect beings.[10] Martin Luther also adopted a utilitar-
ian view, which has prevailed in the West.[11] But like the notion
that the earth only serves human need, the idea that God has no
greater use for animals than to feed humans is neither scriptural
nor, it turns out, sustainable. Nor is it true to the kinship known
between humans and other animals.

Animals as Partners

On the scale of evolutionary time, living with domestic animals
came relatively recently, but long before recorded history. Dogs
were buried with human friends fourteen thousand years ago;
sheep and goats were domesticated about ten thousand years
ago.[12] The variety of roles dogs and cats now play in society
has been expanding as their abilities have become more widely
known. They guide and assist the disabled and mobility impaired.

They comfort children in stressful moments such as court appearances, and live as companions for the elderly in nursing facilities. In one Rhode Island nursing home, a cat named Oscar so accurately senses the approaching death of residents that the staff has learned to call the family when he curls up by a patient.[13]

Wild animals' voluntary contact with humans is also known. From ancient times to now, numerous stories have been told of dolphins rescuing drowning sailors, protecting them from sharks, and guiding ships to safety.[14] Dolphins and sea lions work for the U.S. Navy, detecting underwater mines, guarding harbors and ships, and retrieving objects in the water.

As more becomes known about animal behavior, it is difficult to continue to claim humans as the only creatures possessing self-awareness, love, and choice. Christian theologians today are reconsidering animals' place in religious thinking.[15] The annual blessing of the animals in many churches has dramatically increased awareness of animals as creatures blessed by God. The Church of the New Covenant in Doraville, Georgia, has introduced a Dog Days festival every August, featuring a variety of dog-friendly activities and culminating in a blessing in the sanctuary, in which individual animals are recognized for particular kindness toward their human companions. This popular festival has led many who never knew the church existed to begin worshiping there.

Concentrated Animal Feeding Operations

Ironically, the suffering of both farm animals and those who tend them is increasing. Carole Morison is executive director of the Delmarva Poultry Justice Alliance on the eastern seaboard of Maryland, Delaware, and Virginia. Before this she farmed chickens for more than twenty years. She was honored in 2004 by the Robert Wood Johnson Foundation as a leader in public and environmental health and community development for organizing farmers, religious leaders, workers, and others, to advocate against unfair labor practices and environmental pollution in the poultry industry.

As she explains, most chickens eaten in America today are raised by farm owners like herself, working under contract with Perdue or Tyson, primarily in southeastern states. The farmers provide chicken houses, heating fuel, water, labor, and disposal of manure and dead chickens. But the corporation owns the chicks, which are shipped to the farmer along with food and other "inputs," such as antibiotics.[16] Unlike the little henhouse on Perdue labels, nestling beneath a farmhouse, buildings containing thirty thousand chickens are as large as fifteen human homes, costing the farmer several hundred thousand dollars before any payment is received. Yet annual income may be $8,000, without benefits.[17]

Disposing of daily waste from thirty thousand chickens is more than farmers can manage. In the Delmarva peninsula alone, chickens produce a million tons of manure annually, polluting groundwater and streams. Chicken feed, high in nitrogen, phosphorus, potassium, and heavy metals, encourages speedy, cheap growth. Antibiotics are added to counteract the ill effects of overcrowding and poor ventilation. Like antibiotics fed to cows and other meat animals, these result in ever more resistant strains of bacteria.

Such an industry is part of a much larger recent phenomenon called the "AFO" or "CAFO." The EPA defines Animal Feeding Operations (AFOs) as

> agricultural operations where animals are kept and raised in confined situations. AFOs congregate animals, feed, manure and urine, dead animals, and production operations on a small land area. Feed is brought to the animals rather than the animals grazing or otherwise seeking feed in pastures, fields, or on rangeland.[18]

When the number of animals confined or the degree of pollutants produced exceeds certain levels, the AFO is defined as a Concentrated Animal Feeding Operation (CAFO). A large CAFO includes a thousand or more head of cattle, seven hundred or more dairy cows, twenty-five hundred or more pigs, or thirty thousand or more laying hens.[19]

Such models as these, according to Frederick Kirschenmann, director of the Leopold Center at Iowa State University, exemplify the present and portend the worrisome future of industrial food production, in which "other livestock species and patented seed crops will increasingly be owned by the firm, raised for the firm, in accordance with the firm's management plans, using the firm's technology and inputs."[20] Distant supply chains accrue profits for distant shareholders. Historically creative and independent, farmers become "landowning serfs in an agricultural feudal system."[21]

Losses from this farming style extend beyond farmers to neighbors and the land itself. Farmland cannot absorb that much manure, and becomes degraded. Streams and waterways become polluted. Traditional husbandry dies as farmers are forced to submit to corporate demands. But the greatest losers are the birds themselves, who are debeaked and shipped at one day old, suffering crowded, unventilated conditions for six weeks before being rounded up for slaughter. Modern people like to think our civilization is kinder and gentler than ancient ones, and in some ways it may be. But these practices, neglectful of health, human justice, and animal welfare, would be roundly condemned by Scripture's writers and unrecognizable in traditional cultures.

While the American diet has long centered on meat, never has as much flesh been consumed as today. Veterinarian Michael W. Fox wrote in 1997 that in the United States "7,000 calves, 130,000 cattle, 360,000 pigs, and 24 million chickens are killed every day in order to support a meat-based diet."[22] The methods for growing and butchering each animal differ, but one source after another alleges the following unappetizing conditions:[23]

1. Livestock are grown in overcrowded pens without sunlight, room to move, or ventilation, standing deep in their own manure. Veal calves spend their lives in boxes too small to stand. To keep their meat pale, they are fed diets deficient in iron. Breeding sows are kept in two-foot-wide crates, unable to move or turn around. Egg-laying hens are crowded four to a cage sixteen inches wide, unable to lie down or even stretch their wings. Beef cattle sometimes stand 50,000–100,000 together in dirt yards without shelter or shade.

2. To reduce costs and increase profits, animals are fed inappropriate diets. Bovine digestive tracts are designed for grazing. But corn produced through large doses of natural gas fertilizers, petroleum pesticides, and tax subsidies has proven the cheapest way to fatten them. It also creates serious and sometimes fatal health maladies such as bloat and acidosis. In addition, herbivore livestock are fed parts of dead animals, even of their own species.

3. Because poor diets and overcrowded, stressed conditions incubate disease, animals raised for meat are fed preventive antibiotics. In fact, though the practice is illegal in Europe, in the United States more than three-fourths of all antibiotics produced go to forestalling disease in animals whose conditions make them susceptible.[24]

4. To save money, some animals are starved for days prior to slaughter. Food and water are also withheld from hens for up to two weeks to force egg laying.

5. Animals are subjected to unnecessary pain. Mammals are castrated without anesthesia, beaks of chicks are sheared off; tails of pigs and cattle are cut off; cattle are dehorned and branded in the face with hot irons, all without pain alleviation. When egg-laying hens are hatched, half of them—the male chicks—are discarded, sometimes ground alive or thrown into bins to suffocate.

6. In small farming operations, the pastures on which animals graze are fertilized with their manure, contributing to the land's health. But in CAFOs, manure from several thousand large animals penned together contributes instead to the pollution of land, air, and water. Sewage "lagoons" overflow into streams, contaminating them with fecal bacteria. Methane from animals accounts for more greenhouse gases than the transportation industry.

7. Large amounts of water are wasted. For each pound of pork produced, 430 gallons of water are consumed.[25] Water used for trying to wash fecal matter caked on the carcasses of animals who spent months standing in manure has to go somewhere. It washes into streams, polluting crops and drinking water.

8. Slaughterhouses degrade the health and economic well-being of those who can find no other job, often immigrants.

"Disassembly lines" move dangerously fast, with as many as four hundred cattle an hour moving down one line, where knife-wielding workers must make their cuts quickly and repetitively.[26] These nonunionized employees are pressured not to report their injuries. Governmental oversight has been lax.

9. Though privately owned, these operations receive government subsidies for pesticides, irrigation, animal feed, and waste management. Citizens also pay for environmental cleanup. Neighbors of factory farms pay not only in farm loss from direct competition with larger operations, but in lost property value and degraded health. Organizing and petitions rarely result in denial of permits.

10. Consumers pay in poorer nutrition. Diets rich in fat, cholesterol, and animal protein increase risks of obesity, heart disease, colon cancer, arteriosclerosis, gout, and other diseases. Potentially fatal diseases from contaminants include salmonella and E.coli poisoning and Creutzfeldt-Jakob Disease, the human variant of mad cow disease.

11. Factory farming has spread to poorer countries exporting meat to the United States. Large-scale cattle ranching in Central America has cost millions of acres of tropical forests. Many of these exporting countries cannot feed their own children.

A 2003 survey of veterinarians across the nation betrayed deep objections to practices enumerated above.[27] Many commented that part of what drives the industry is consumer demand for low-cost meat and lack of knowledge about its production. Ironically, the more industrialized meat has become, the less it resembles animals: boneless, skinless breasts or even chicken nuggets shaped like rectangles or dinosaurs are the only poultry some consumers know.

The many allegations concerning the conditions in which animals are grown and butchered, the environmental losses and dangers to which this practice exposes both us and the land, the health hazards of too much meat and of factory-farmed meat, and the social and economic degradation of those who work in these environments are causes for grave concern. The United States faces major problems—environmental and moral—that churches could and should be addressing. For many people of faith who experience a sense of God's tender love, it is difficult to imagine giving thanks in a table blessing for the tissue of a mute beast whose entire life—not just its final day—was endured in misery. It is painful to consider what the God who called the teeming creation good, and who directed Israelites to take pity on the suffering of even their enemies' animals, must think about factory farming.

Christians take comfort in reciting, "The LORD is my shepherd, I shall not want" (Ps. 23:1). In this psalm we identify ourselves with grazing farm animals for whom the Great Shepherd provides water, pasturage, comfort, and restoration. To invoke such a psalm for ourselves while dining on animals who lacked such safety under our rule seems cold.

Alternative Pathways

The description of human care for flocks in Proverbs 27:23–27 provides a corollary to Psalm 23, prescribing attentiveness to the needs of the animals who provide wool and milk:

> Know well the condition of your flocks,
>   and give attention to your herds;
> for riches do not last forever,
>   nor a crown for all generations.
> When the grass is gone, and new growth appears,
>   and the herbage of the mountains is gathered,
> the lambs will provide your clothing,
>   and the goats the price of a field;
> there will be enough goats' milk for your food,
>   for the food of your household
>   and nourishment for your servant-girls.

Barbara Kingsolver, whose family raises their own meat, describes their ethical path:

> In '97, when our family gave up meat from CAFOs, that choice was synonymous with becoming a vegetarian. No real

alternatives existed. Now they do. Pasture-based chicken and turkey are available in whole food stores and many mainstream supermarkets. Farmers' markets are a likely source for free-range eggs, poultry, beef, lamb, and pork.[28]

Joel Salatin owns Polyface Farms in Virginia's Shenandoah Valley. His guiding principles include transparency to the public, respect for animals, sustainable pasturing, and selling his meats only locally. His model of pasture rotation has been replicated on countless other small farms. Cattle are moved almost daily. After them comes a portable henhouse from which chickens range, scratching through and spreading the cattle droppings to fertilize the field. Pigs, turkeys, broilers, and rabbits are similarly fed diets appropriate to their biology and ecological niche. Salatin says his animals have one bad day in their lives.

Novelist Jonathan Safran Foer chose a different approach. Despite deep familial memories associated with eating meat, he and his family became vegetarian:

> According to an analysis of U.S.D.A. data by the advocacy group Farm Forward, factory farms now produce more than 99 percent of the animals eaten in this country. And despite labels that suggest otherwise, genuine alternatives—which do exist, and make many of the ethical questions about meat moot—are very difficult for even an educated eater to find. I don't have the ability to do so with regularity and confidence.[29]

Meat raised humanely on unsubsidized, smaller farms is more expensive than the products of corner-cutting CAFOs. Complaints about this are largely unrealistic, however, since in the United States we have managed to decrease the percentage of household budgets spent on groceries from almost 50 percent a century ago to 10 percent today, while dramatically increasing our per capita meat intake.[30] Still, there are affordable ways to adapt. Some families go meatless, satisfying protein needs with legumes and grains. Others eat smaller portions, loading plates with vegetables and fruits. Still others follow the lead of our ancestors, eating meat less frequently. To eat meat with integrity is to confront the question of how we "farm by proxy," to acknowledge what meat is, and at what costs it comes to us. Though each person's conscience operates differently, our eating should bear continuity with our principles.

Is factory farming necessary, given the world's growing population, as some argue? Can we only urge industries to curb the worst abuses? Well-informed debates are needed among all stake-holders—growers, agribusinesses, grocers, restaurants, eaters, and all who live on a planet increasingly harmed by this practice. A report concerning differences between CAFO industry claims and documented realities was prepared by William J. Weida, a retired Air Force economist.[31] This report examines nineteen claims, and in each case reveals, with extensive documentation, the realities undermining these claims. Weida invites permitting agencies and rural residents to hold industries accountable. Efficiency of scale is a particularly interesting discussion, raising questions about the inevitability of factory farming for meeting human needs.

It takes more than changes in individual daily habits, or even in whole communities and cities, to reform a system buttressed by corporate wealth and federal legislation. The large farm bills passed every five to seven years affect not only farming but also local food systems and food security, labor practices, grocery prices, energy, public health, land conservation, ecological health, international trade, and world hunger. Everyone who eats has a stake in this legislation, and everyone has the right and responsibility to speak out about its use of our tax dollars.[32]

News stories occasionally reveal the power of public opinion. In November 2011, ABC's *20/20* aired a program showing videos made covertly inside Sparboe Farms egg factory in Iowa. This investigation of regular and exceptional animal cruelty and public health threats led to FDA censures and cancellation of large contracts by Target and McDonald's, for whom Sparboe was the sole egg supplier west of the Mississippi.[33] Recognizing the damage of such information to their images, these two companies quickly distanced themselves from this mega-supplier.

Human Attraction to Animals

Once in Montana I saw a crowd of tourists gathering on the dock outside a restaurant, passing binoculars back and forth, pointing to a speck across the water. We had all had closer views of grizzlies at zoos, but to see one roaming freely, even in the distance, changed what the land was and who inhabited it. In the North Woods of Wisconsin, my husband and I sat by a lake reading. We went inside for just a moment, and saw through the picture window, almost close enough to touch, a black bear and two cubs eating platefuls of bird seed we had set out. We had been warned about this bear. Yet we felt graced with special privilege when she came.

We've had rabbits in the garage and opossums in the compost. Once in broad daylight a raccoon opened the screen door and peered in at us as if asking when was tea. A goose wandered from the river and stood on the patio looking perplexed till our ten-year-old walked it home. Hawks on road signs; ground hogs by overpasses; herons on the docks; sandhill cranes flying in formation; cormorants standing on the shore and swimming like up periscopes, barely seen beneath the bridge, diving and reappearing; robins raising young on our front porch; geese so steadfast in their place that we could watch their children grow from week to week; chipmunks, crickets, finches; foxes stealing out from tree lines and quickly disappearing; even in the city, other worlds intersect with ours, and ours is larger for it.

Walking by the Ohio River one night near dark, I saw a shape slide from a rock into the water, disappear momentarily, and then form two round humps, a head and a back, paddling first in a circle and then downstream. I followed. Once or twice it looked up. Then it climbed up on a rock, its body silhouetted by the river. With its paws it pulled up weeds from cracks between the rocks. As the light grew dimmer I crept close and knelt on the grass six feet away. The sound of chewing, magnified by the water, made the beaver seem even nearer, as if we were in the same room, at the same table. It chewed the weeds for several minutes and then, without a word between us, slid into the river and paddled on downstream.

Episcopalian contemplative Susan Mangam tells of an encounter in a field with a cow for whom she was searching. She had often observed cows presenting their newborn calves to the herd, allowing others to greet the newcomer with a gentle sniff. This time, though, it is she herself who is first to receive the cow's ritual act of courtesy, and finds herself humbled and honored by this recognition.[34] Matthew Scully tells stories of two terrified pigs who escape execution by scuttling under a fence and swimming an icy river, and of one pig who saved its owner from death during a heart attack by lying in the road until a car stopped, and leading the stranger to the house.[35]

Is it really only sentiment that makes us love the animals? Is it speciated loneliness, hunger for greeting from beyond the human, which we feel deeply but want to ignore? Or is it recognition, though we cannot speak their language, that other animals feel pain and desire, possess intelligence, agency, dignity, value of their own, significance for us? If our own prayers could more frankly approach those attributed to the fourth-century saint Basil the Great of Caesarea, our attention might well be drawn to their grace:

> O God, enlarge within us the sense of fellowship with all living things, our brothers the animals to whom Thou gavest the earth as their home in common with us. We remember with shame that in the past we have exercised the high dominion of man with ruthless cruelty so that the voice of the earth, which should have gone up to Thee in song has been a groan of travail. May we realize that they live not for us alone, but for themselves and for Thee and that they love the sweetness of life even as we, and serve Thee better in their place than we in ours.
>
> For those, O Lord, the humble beasts, that bear with us the burden and heat of day . . . and for the wild creatures, whom Thou hast made wise, strong, and beautiful, we supplicate for them Thy great tenderness of heart, for Thou hast promised to save both man and beast, and great is Thy loving kindness, O Master, Saviour of the world.[36]

According to Scripture, God enjoins self-limitation and self-control. Sinai laws teach kindness and respect toward animals. As a society, the ways we choose our food, what and how and where and from whom we decide to eat each day, shapes the nature of the garden overall, the U.S. farming landscape, the good earth we were called to serve and preserve. Even if we work in a cubicle in a skyscraper and go home to an urban apartment, at least three times a day we make choices concerning our first vocation. To assure that our eating is healthful and just takes effort. But like other efforts, it builds habits reflecting our values, habits that may heal our relationships with the larger world around us.

Questions for Thought and Discussion

1. Which biblical images of humans as animals, or human relations to animals, stand out most to you? What do they mean to you?
2. What is your instinctive feeling about animals, whether household, farm, or wild? Do you remember special relationships with animals, or feelings for them, as children? What experiences have you had with animals?
3. Do you remember your own or someone else's reaction to the realization that meat was animal flesh? What was that like?
4. What is meat's place in your meals? How often do you eat it, and in what proportions? Has this changed over time?
5. How does our treatment of animals affect our relationships with God and other humans?

Try This at Home

Read Exodus 19:4; Deuteronomy 32:11–14; Psalms 84:3 and 103:5; Isaiah 31:5, 40:31, and Luke 13:34. Write down what is being said about animals in these passages.

Spend an hour or two in the presence of animals wherever you might find them: in a zoo, on a farm, in the countryside, or in your backyard. Observe their behavior and settings. What life functions do you see them carrying out (eating, drinking, caring for young, courting, grooming, playing, and so forth)? If you could understand their speech, what do you imagine them communicating? If you have children, be sure to include them in this venture.

If your family eats meat, dairy, or eggs, learn where you can find producers committed to the welfare of land, animals, and workers. How do prices compare? How might a meal—or a week's menu—be planned that neither uses CAFO products nor raises your grocery budget? If it raises your budget unavoidably, how much increase is acceptable for conscience's sake?

Give the king your justice, O God,
    and your righteousness to a king's son.
  . . . .
May the mountains yield prosperity for the people,
    and the hills, in righteousness.
May he defend the cause of the poor of the people,
    give deliverance to the needy,
    and crush the oppressor.

—Psalm 72:1, 3–4

Automobile fuel economy is an environmental issue. But when our dependence on cheap gasoline drives a tanker aground, and the spreading slick deprives an Inuit family of seal meat, that's an issue of justice and compassion.

Recycling is an environmental issue. But when a Chicago woman who's never smoked cigarettes gets lung cancer from breathing fumes from an incinerator burning recyclable trash, that's an issue of justice and compassion.

Deforestation is an environmental issue. But when tree root systems no longer hold soil in place and a mudslide sweeps away a peasant village, that's an issue of justice and compassion.

—Fred Small, "The Greater Sacrifice,"
in *Love God, Heal Earth*

Chapter 7

Environmental Fairness

Vineyard Stories

The neighborhood of palaces may seem like an ideal place to live. But it turns out not to be so for Naboth, an Israelite living in Samaria in the ninth century BCE. It starts with a business offer. "'Give me your vineyard, so that I may have it for a vegetable garden, because it is near my house,'" King Ahab says. "'I will give you a better vineyard for it; or, if it seems good to you, I will give you its value in money'" (1 Kgs. 21:2). Ahab's father Omri had built the city of Samaria similarly, by buying property from Shemer, paying him well and naming the new town after him.

But Naboth wants to keep his vineyard. He calls it his "ancestral heritage" (v. 3), a phrase filled with reminders of God's gift of land. The vineyard is his family's, his household's piece of the world. He intends to give it to his children and their children. So he refuses.

That could have been the end of it, or Ahab could have returned with a better offer. But the king goes home nursing an unroyal sulk, and his supportive wife Jezebel gets involved. She cheerfully tells Ahab to buck up. She will take care of Naboth:

> She wrote letters in Ahab's name and sealed them with his seal; she sent the letters to the elders and the nobles who

111

lived with Naboth in his city. She wrote in the letters, "Proclaim a fast, and seat Naboth at the head of the assembly; seat two scoundrels opposite him, and have them bring a charge against him, saying, 'You have cursed God and the king.' Then take him out, and stone him to death." The men of his city, the elders and the nobles who lived in his city, did as Jezebel had sent word to them. Just as it was written in the letters that she had sent to them, they proclaimed a fast and seated Naboth at the head of the assembly. The two scoundrels came in and sat opposite him; and the scoundrels brought a charge against Naboth, in the presence of the people, saying, "Naboth cursed God and the king." So they took him outside the city, and stoned him to death. Then they sent to Jezebel, saying, "Naboth has been stoned; he is dead."

As soon as Jezebel heard that Naboth had been stoned and was dead, Jezebel said to Ahab, "Go, take possession of the vineyard of Naboth the Jezreelite, which he refused to give you for money; for Naboth is not alive, but dead." As soon as Ahab heard that Naboth was dead, Ahab set out to go down to the vineyard of Naboth the Jezreelite, to take possession of it. (1 Kgs. 21:8–16)

Jezebel's cynical instructions suggest imparting to the proceedings an air of outraged piety. The elders comply with the government, achieve the desired result, and report back: the deed is done; the troublemaker is gone; religious sensibilities are appeased; the neighborhood is open for development. The only catch is that God holds Ahab and Jezebel accountable, and they both meet horrible ends predicted by the prophet Elijah (21:17–24). Ahab goes to battle disguised as a commoner and is killed (22:29–38). Jezebel's own servants toss her from a window (2 Kgs. 9:30–37). Dogs consume Ahab's blood and Jezebel's body.

The storyteller's mocking tone diminishes the royal couple's fearsomeness. They are dangerous, deadly bullies, but to hear the writer tell it, scratch their surfaces and you find a childish king and an avaricious queen, both of them self-consumed. Their aim wasn't to kill Naboth; he was just standing in their way. He was collateral damage. We hear no more about the vegetable garden. Like many things keenly desired, its value no doubt diminishes the moment Ahab takes it, replaced by some other want.

What is horrifying is not this selfish couple, but Naboth's vividness, drawn in a few sentences. To see someone before he dies, to know his name, to hear him speak, gains us a glimpse of his soul. And it doesn't take more to know that his life is much bigger than we see. To watch him silenced after one sentence, one moment that some might call a political misstep and others an act of uncommon courage, muted before public tribunal—that is the horror. Someone we never knew fills the page, and then is snuffed out.

But the matter doesn't end there. This happened in the northern kingdom of Israel. The story passes into the lore of Judah to the south. Yet Jerusalem's nobility learn so little that later prophets charge them with similar crimes. Isaiah 5:1–7 tells another vineyard story, one in which God's vineyard itself grows bad fruit. It concludes with these words:

> For the vineyard of the LORD of hosts
>   is the house of Israel,
> and the people of Judah
>   are the seedlings in which God delighted.
> God expected justice (Hebrew: *mishpat*),
>   but there was bloodshed (*mishpah*);
> righteousness (*tsedakah*),
>   but there was an outcry (*tse'akah*)!
> (Isa. 5:7, AT)

This contrast between God's desire and Israel's deed is not a casual comment in Isaiah. The book pairs these two words, "justice" and "righteousness" (or as some translate them together, "social justice"), nine other times (Isa. 1:27; 5:16; 9:7; 28:17; 32:1, 16; 33:5; 59:9, 14), and mentions justice nineteen additional times besides these. For this prophet, as for others, social justice signifies love for God.

Immediately after this indictment, the prophet begins and ends a series of seven condemnations of greed with words that further remind us of Ahab and Jezebel, both their taking of land and their perverting of law:

> Woe to those who add house to house,
>   who join field to field
> until there is no space left
>   and you live alone in the midst of the land.
> (Isa. 5:8, AT)

> Woe to those who decree wicked decrees,
>   and keep writing harmful laws
> to deprive the needy of their rights
>   and to steal justice from my people's poor,
> to make widows their spoil,
>   to plunder orphans!
> (Isa. 10:1–2, AT)

The horror here is the opposite of that in Naboth's story. Here the needy, poor, widows, and orphans cannot come to life for us. We don't see individuals; we don't learn their names; we don't hear them speak. They aren't even statistics. Whatever led Isaiah to speak for them is lost, and we must fill in the blanks with possibilities. If we don't imagine all the way up to Naboth's death, we trivialize their tragedies.

If we know anything about our faith, we know the Bible's vehemence on God's love, specifically for "the least of these." This message extends from Sinai laws protecting orphans and widows to Jesus' parable about feeding the hungry, welcoming the stranger, clothing the naked, nursing the sick, and visiting the prisoner, the one that concludes with "just as you did it (or did not do it) to one of the least of these who are members of my family, you did it (or did not do it) to me" (Matt. 25:40, 45). This central teaching of both the Old and New Testaments has inspired Christian social services throughout the centuries, from widows' pensions in Acts to hospitals, schools, farm projects, immigrant services, food pantries, clothes closets, and prison ministries today. We get the part about caring for those whose lives are precarious.

Environmental justice enters the picture wherever harms to the poor result from other people's destruction of land, water, and air, jeopardizing their lives and livelihood, as Naboth's land and life were stolen from him. Some people are relatively more able to protect themselves from environmental hazards. Others, because of poverty, geography, youth, or old age, do not enjoy the same protections.

Several issues raised in previous chapters involve environmental justice. The transformation of stores into big boxes by industries that decrease prices by externalizing the ecological and human costs of manufacturing has reduced many adults to being minimum-wage earners in insecure jobs. Food production employees, from field workers to meatpackers, suffer conditions that destroy lives, health, and families. Rural neighbors of factory farms suffer ecological damage and depressed real estate values. The use of electricity created from coal, discussed in chapter 3, involves multiple dimensions of human fairness, both rural and urban: from the destruction of health, homes, and habitat that often accompanies mining (especially such radical practices as mountaintop removal) to the emission of mercury and creation of coal ash by coal-fired electrical plants, which are usually found closest to poor neighborhoods. All of these problems share both ecological and justice dimensions. Given the political will, they could all be resolved.

While environmental justice takes many forms, this chapter will reflect specifically on the modern Naboths who lose property and even health and life to more powerful neighbors, specifically to industries nearby whose toxic waste invades their air, water, soil, and bodies. They become our unseen collateral damage, rarely making the news. Their communities become the "sacrifice zones" that enable others to enjoy inexpensive products. Or as one resident near oil refineries in Port Arthur, Texas, put it, "Our neighborhood pays the price for the rest of the nation's cheap gas."[1]

Trampling Sheep

More than a century after Isaiah, and longer after Naboth's death
than the United States has yet existed, the prophet Ezekiel, exiled
to Babylon, seeks to understand what went wrong in Jerusalem,
what led to Judah's recent destruction. Ezekiel draws a grim picture. He calls Jerusalem a "bloody city," treating parents with contempt, extorting from foreigners, wronging widows and orphans,
taking bribes. He calls the city's leaders roaring lions tearing their
prey, devouring, stealing, destroying lives for dishonest gain. No
one can accuse Ezekiel of soft-pedaling. Extreme times call for
honest assessment. He names many direct crimes, but in chapter
34 he also names indirect crimes:

> As for you, my flock, thus says the Lord GOD: I shall judge
> between sheep and sheep, between rams and goats: Is it not
> enough for you to feed on the good pasture, but you must
> tread down with your feet the rest of your pasture? When
> you drink of clear water, must you foul the rest with your
> feet? And must my sheep eat what you have trodden with
> your feet, and drink what you have fouled with your feet?
>
> Therefore, thus says the Lord GOD to them: I myself
> will judge between the fat sheep and the lean sheep.
> Because you pushed with flank and shoulder, and butted
> at all the weak animals with your horns until you scattered
> them far and wide, I will save my flock, and they shall no
> longer be ravaged; and I will judge between sheep and
> sheep. (Ezek. 34:17–22)

Here the crimes Ezekiel names are largely indirect: spoiling land
and water so that others can no longer eat and drink; ruining the
resources others rely on for no better reason than heedless greed.
The prophet's accusations contrast sharply with human vocation
as Genesis describes, serving and preserving God's garden.

What rights do we believe all people have? Do they have the
right, like Naboth, to preserve land their ancestors developed and
passed on to them? Do they have the right not to be deprived of

its use, or even killed, for others' convenience? The right to their day in court, and a legal system that defends their interests? Do they have the same rights we do to life's necessities—food, water, breathable air, a safe living environment? Questions such as these, central to our religious tradition, stand at the nexus between ecological and human rights issues.

Once again, the question here is not whether Scripture yields exact parallels to contemporary dilemmas. Rather it is the extent to which we are at least living up to Scripture's best principles. If we find Scripture instructive, and even authoritative, how might we encourage better practices for our world? How might the poor live well on their often small bits of land, and enjoy as much health as others can? When they seek legal protection, do the courts listen? What does our faith say about our role?

Environmental Justice

Environmental justice is not only consistent with biblical values. It has also become our nation's standard. According to the U.S. Environmental Protection Agency:

> Environmental Justice is the fair treatment and meaningful involvement of all people regardless of race, color, national origin, or income with respect to the development, implementation, and enforcement of environmental laws, regulations, and policies. Fair treatment means that no group of people should bear a disproportionate share of the negative environmental consequences resulting from industrial, governmental, and commercial operations or policies. Meaningful involvement means that: (1) people have an opportunity to participate in decisions about activities that may affect their environment and/or health; (2) the public's contribution can influence the regulatory agency's decision; (3) their concerns will be considered in the decision making process; and (4) the decision makers seek out and facilitate the involvement of those potentially affected.[2]

The EPA works "to provide an environment where all people enjoy the same degree of protection from ecological and health hazards and equal access to the decision-making process to maintain a healthy environment in which to live, learn, and work."[3]

These protections were hard won. We've written them into law, but now we must close gaps between law and practice. Just as smoking may be a choice, but secondary smoke harms others, when toxic emissions harm neighbors without their choice, the concern is not lifestyle but public health.

In this chapter and the next we will explore two specific topics. Both involve indirect destruction of human health and life through direct—even when unintended—degradation of land, water, and air. These problems can be addressed only partly by individual ecological choices. They often involve corporations with larger economies than many whole countries, whose industries are so fully woven into the national and international fabric that opting out would mean opting out of society. One would have to leave the energy grid, refuse medical services, travel by foot, and produce much of one's own food and nearly all of one's own goods, while still earning sufficient money to cover the increased costs of these changes—or, if one were lucky enough to live from personal wealth, find investments that didn't benefit from these same business practices.

In other words, in today's world, we cannot choose *whether* we participate in environmental injustice, but we can change *how* we participate in this morally ambiguous economic web, a web at odds with, and damaging to, the web of God's creation. We can't leave this web, but we can transform it, making changes, mostly incremental ones, in the culture itself.

In this chapter we will discuss toxic waste, and in chapter 8, greenhouse gases. While the first danger is more immediate, the second looms larger. There is much bad news here. The good news is that we have far more potential to change society than we have tapped, and that changes are already in motion.

Toxic Pollutants

Dr. Kristin Shrader-Frechette teaches environmental biology and ethics at Notre Dame University. She has served on the EPA's science advisory board and has advised the Centers for Disease Control, NASA, and the Department of Energy, as well as several foreign governments and the U.N., the World Health Organization, and the World Council of Churches. She directs the Center for Environmental Justice and Children's Health, where professors and students work pro bono with community groups worldwide to assess ecological health dangers and inform residents of their rights and risks. She has written much on environmental pollutants for a wide reading audience, from scientists to the rest of us.

Shrader-Frechette points out the health risks of industrial pollutants, especially to children's vulnerable and fast-growing bodies.[4] She argues that because we benefit from products whose manufacture generates pollutants, "ordinary citizens have ethical responsibilities to use traditional democratic tools to help prevent threats to life and health."[5] Estimates from the U.S. National Cancer Institute show industrial pollution contributing to sixty thousand premature American cancer deaths annually—three times more than murders.[6] Cancer is the leading cause of death for women in their thirties.[7] According to the U.S. Office of Technology Assessment, "Up to ninety percent of cancers are environmentally induced and theoretically preventable."[8]

But it's not just cancer. Heart disease, asthma and other respiratory ailments, endocrine disruption, genetic defects, birth defects, neurological and other developmental disorders, lung disease, atherosclerosis, allergies, and sudden infant death syndrome are also linked to environmental pollutants. Particulate air pollution causes 6.4 percent of all deaths among young children in developed nations, and about ten percent of all deaths in Chicago alone, about three thousand each year. More than twenty-six countries have better air quality than the United States.

According to the *New England Journal of Medicine*, Shrader-Frechette explains, environmental pollutants play a large role in childhood cancers. Each year, 12,500 children are diagnosed and half of them die—twice as many as in auto accidents. Page after page spells out not only statistics concerning toxins from factories, coal plants, oil refineries, waste incinerators, and automobiles, but also the excruciating stories of families and whole communities unwittingly subjected to compromised health simply because of where they can afford to live.

While throughout society increased exposure to toxins is coinciding with increased cancers and other ailments, the greatest harm falls on the poor, who are often exposed through factory jobs and whose neighborhoods disproportionately become move-in sites for polluting industries: "incinerators, hazardous waste dumps, refineries, gasoline tank farms, plastic plants, steel mills, pesticide plants, cement kilns, sewage treatment plants, rubber factories, asphalt batching plants, large-scale pig and cattle feedlots, agricultural areas heavily sprayed with pesticides, tanneries, machine shops, auto-crushing-and-shredding operations."[9] Such locally unwanted land uses, or LULUs, move in where land is cheaper and zoning poorer. The strange zoning category "residential/industrial" means there is little breathing space between smokestacks and children at play.[10] Neighbors of factories are often too overworked and under-informed to protest.

These same neighbors can scarcely afford the preventive health care that keeps bodies more resistant. When they fall sick and seek emergency room treatment, taxpayers share the cost. The greatest harm falls on children, whose young bodies absorb many times more chemicals than adult bodies. So the fifteen million U.S. children below the poverty line are doubly endangered.[11]

Steve Lerner brings the problem down to the Naboth level. He traveled to twelve different communities throughout the United States to learn from neighbors who have tried, with varying success, to protect their communities from harms ranging from ash to oil spills to dioxins.[12] Though they may be poor, underserved, and often sick, and though they often find themselves rebuffed by manufacturers and civic leaders, some residents persist over the course of years, documenting the presence of toxins and the prevalence of unusual diseases, researching the links between them, speaking out at hearings and meetings, drawing media attention, and negotiating for remediation or relocation.

In the course of their efforts, residents often discover even more distressing information. A poor and mostly black Pensacola community suffered from 1944 to 1982 from groundwater poisoning by a company treating lumber with creosote and, later, pentachlorophenol (PCP), a biocide.[13] Wastewater dumped into unlined holes seeped into their wells. During storms, factory chemicals poured into yards and homes.

After the plant closed in 1982, the EPA declared it a Superfund site. "Superfund" is an environmental program established after Love Canal to clean up abandoned hazardous waste sites, whenever possible compelling responsible parties to perform the cleanup themselves or to reimburse the government for the work.[14] Thirteen hundred sites are presently on the EPA's priority list. One-third of these polluters can't be found or can't pay, so cleanup cost is borne by taxpayers. This cost was originally paid by the petroleum and chemical industries, but is no longer.[15]

While other Superfund cleanups have succeeded, this one went badly. As contractors excavated PCP-contaminated soil, estimates of the contamination's extent kept rising. After spending $5 million, and facing a hundred million dollars more, officials gave up on removal and tried covering the soil instead. Throughout these efforts, residents were left unshielded and suffered respiratory distress, nosebleeds, headaches, nausea, and skin rashes. They tried to stop the digging. When their efforts failed, they asked for relocation. Comparable homes had cost $135,000, but, because of the contamination itself, first estimates of their home values ranged from $20,000 to $27,000. During negotiations, residents learned that homeowners in a suburban Pennsylvania community, relocated because of radiation, were given custom-built homes costing four times the appraised value of comparable unpolluted homes. Though the Pensacola residents never received such endowments, their relocation became the third largest in U.S.

history. Leaving behind lifelong neighborhood ties, they found their victory bittersweet.

By the time a Superfund site is declared, the polluter is often long gone. But negotiating with an industry that is still emitting toxins can be just as disheartening. In Addyston, Ohio, a plastics plant operated across the street from an elementary school, causing headaches, stomach pains, and absenteeism, forcing residents to close the school in 2005. The factory resisted taking responsibility for frequent accidental, underreported emissions of carcinogens such as acrylonitrile and butadiene. Residents, who could smell the chemicals and were often sickened by them, began monitoring the air themselves, using five-gallon buckets, plastic liners, and air pumps. In 2006, what residents knew anecdotally was verified statistically: their cancer rate was 76 percent higher than the general population's, and lung cancer was four times higher. At that point, state EPA officials began to hold the factory accountable.[16]

If dangers from toxic pollution are both widespread and scientifically well-known, why isn't this on the news every day? Or as Shrader-Frechette puts it, "Why do news reports give relatively little attention to pollution-induced childhood diseases like cancers, although they kill more children than automobiles, murder, or child abuse combined?"[17] Given the EPA's environmental justice standards, how can this happen at all? And why must people spend time, money, energy, and agony fighting these diseases person by person if they could be prevented?

Epidemics in Slow Motion

When a tornado rages, no one wonders why people died. Cause and effect are instantaneously linked. Unlike polluting industries, tornadoes cannot hire attorneys to contend that victims' lifestyles endangered them. But when toxic effects take decades to appear, cause and effect are much more difficult to prove. Cancer is "an epidemic in slow motion," made all the more insidious by the complexity of studying its links with environmental factors.[18] Potential hazards are generally deemed "innocent until proven guilty," as if these products were human beings. What is more, as sociologist Phil Brown notes, by the time even circumstantial evidence begins linking cause and effect, an industry is so well established that its contributions seem irreplaceable, and its monetary resources become quite powerful. The tobacco and lead paint industries both marshaled massive financial and political support, calling scientific studies into question and manufacturing ambiguities and controversies for decades.[19] In fact, it took the United States until 1970 to ban lead, half a century behind many other countries.

Brown and others advocate a precautionary principle: "When an activity raises threats of harm to human health or the environment, precautionary measures should be taken even if some cause and effect relationships are not fully established scientifically."[20] Under this principle, the burden of proof lies not on those being harmed by a substance already on the market, but on the product's sponsors. The approach is preventive. Though prudent, this principle is not immediately profitable for industries. It will take a major shift in public attitudes to make such a principle the norm in the United States as it is in Europe.

Shrader-Frechette emphasizes the chasm between fact and public awareness. Over several decades, large polluting corporations have developed means to keep sensitive information from view. They "capture" regulatory agencies through large campaign donations, and through revolving doors between government service and industry employment so that policing officials are past and often future corporate employees. They buy news media, insist on self-policing, and ruin reputations and even lives of investigators and whistleblowers. Scientists are encouraged by industry-funded research grants and private-interest "think tanks" to engage in research favoring their interests.[21] We have heard all this, but the slivers of news stories are usually disconnected from broader implications.

Though Shrader-Frechette helps readers understand better why crucial information does not flow unimpeded, she is not simply placing blame. These realities make the work of democracy more difficult, she says, but they do not excuse citizens from responsibility to know and act. "Ultimately," she says, "health threats do not arise merely because of ineffectual regulators or a few corporations who behave unethically. They arise because people themselves do not play the role in democracy that they ought to play."[22]

Some people attempt to pit ecological concerns against economics, claiming that to clean up land, air, or water, to preserve the habitat of endangered species, or to build sustainable energy systems costs too much. But in fact most practices that endanger nonhumans also endanger humans, and most practices that are healthy for nonhumans also benefit us. Paul Templet, a retired professor of environmental science at Louisiana State University, ran Louisiana's Department of Environmental Quality in the late 1980s, when Louisiana had the country's highest levels of toxic chemical releases. Within four years he cut emissions in half. In an interview on Public Radio International's *Living on Earth*, he reflected, "Previous governors have said we have to sacrifice the environment to get jobs—we now know that was a Faustian bargain. . . . Now we know that you've got to have a good environment to have a good business climate."[23] He spent the next ten years researching the relationship between economics and ecological cleanup and discovered that though manufacturers threatened job losses, evidence indicated the opposite. Since pollution control enforcement created jobs, moved commerce, and provided more attractive living environments, states with strong environmental programs had stronger economies.[24] Subsequent studies continue to find the same.

Shrader-Frechette advocates a small-wins approach. She cites numerous examples in which concerned people join or form organizations to address local concerns.[25] The goal is not just external change but the experience that transforms individuals into effective citizens, people who, having seen successes, enjoy hope. Small wins provide information that can be channeled into the next step and help citizens to become more hardy—to develop a sense of purpose, to learn to accept and even enjoy challenges. Our instincts may lead us to passivity or to passionate but uninformed action. Every task is most effectively broken into steps:

1. Become informed through critical, discerning reading.
2. Work with others through civil rights groups, church groups, and professional societies.
3. Evaluate health threats and solutions. What are the facts? How have others approached similar issues? What laws are available and what democratic tools are appropriate? What approaches to promoting public awareness might turn the tide, making a practice people did not know or question into a matter of debate? Here especially, particular areas of professional expertise become helpful.
4. Organize and carry out sustained personal and collective action: surveys, data collection, advocacy, attending public hearings, contacting public officials, meeting with polluters, or litigation.

Shrader-Frechette's book and Web site offer many other suggestions.[26] She emphasizes that this is not charity, but the responsibility incurred by those reaping benefits from harmful industries.

Action can be complicated not only by factory owners' interests, but by residents' differing opinions. Jobs can be lost if a factory closes or moves. But community action to stop or prevent pollution need not take an adversarial course. Public education and deliberation, well dosed with communication, can allow people to act on conviction without antagonism.

The moving documentary film *Deep Down: A Story from the Heart of Coal Country*, directed by Jen Gilomen and Sally Rubin, shows an eastern Kentucky community working through divisions when a coal company offers one resident what at first seems like a handsome sum for a mining lease on his land—land adjacent to that of neighbors who have refused, and whose intergenerational heritage is threatened with ruin by mountaintop removal. Though the issue, like the mining method itself, is explosive and violent, the residents face one another courageously, holding hands, so to speak, as they debate.

In that Appalachian community the debate is partly theological. Samuel Maggard, the company's vice president, maintains that "God put coal and other natural resources here for a purpose.

That purpose is for energy requirements and jobs." But resident Beverly May says, "There's a document at the county courthouse that says I own twenty-one acres on Wilson Creek. But I don't think I own it. . . . It is mine to take care of, and to protect, and to enjoy, and then to pass on to the next generation—hopefully in better shape than I got it." The film shows neighbors not only debating but also playing music and eating together, listening, worrying over consequences, and finally reaching understanding, saving their mountain and strengthening their ties. Where a community deliberates well, modern Naboths and their ancestral land are saved.

Christian Commitment to Justice

Shrader-Frechette bases her arguments on democracy. People of faith have a further layer of authority: we do justice because it's our religious ethic. We are with Elijah, not Ahab and Jezebel. We are on Isaiah's and Ezekiel's side. We had rather be those who gave for the least of these than those who gave excuses. We had rather enter the joy of God's realm, not just after death, but while on earth.

Christian denominations often write position papers addressing injustices nationally or worldwide. In 1987 the United Church of Christ published "Toxic Wastes and Race in the United States: A National Report on the Racial and Socio-Economic Characteristics of Communities with Hazardous Waste Sites," and since then other church groups have followed.[27] As helpful as such documents may be, a "think globally, act locally" ethic makes sense. Conditions in each distressed community are unique to the geographical setting and type of industry involved.[28] Individual congregations can play key roles, working with neighbors to research issues, publicize problems, and negotiate solutions. Some churches even tailor their approach to members' expertise, such as medical, legal, or educational competencies.

Many environmental justice groups offer tours of toxic zones. Recently some of us joined a tour of Rubbertown in west Louisville, where nearly half of the county's industrial emissions originate. Once filled with truck farms, it began its industrial life with oil refineries in the early twentieth century. Today, compounds from eleven industries contribute to many products, from disposable diapers to rocket boosters. Two coal-fired power plants also operate in west Louisville, and a third directly across the river in Indiana.[29] Homes have been contaminated by coal ash blowing from one plant's "high hazard" ash pond and landfill. All this had been in the news, but it was different to go, smell the air, and see the proximity of these operations to homes where Naboths lived. Along with a tour of Appalachian coal mining towns, it was a first step for congregation members to see the repercussions for ourselves.

While individual lifestyle changes cannot sufficiently address toxic pollution, Kentucky Interfaith Power and Light director Tim Darst notes that consumer choices do matter. A bottle of water is not only exorbitantly costly and statistically unlikely to be recycled, but its petroleum-based plastic container was manufactured in someone else's neighborhood, degrading their air quality. Attention to the chemicals in products we buy benefits both our family and the factory workers and neighbors close to their production. As we seek to know where the products on our shelves originated, through what processes, and at what costs, we become better educated. No manufacturer will say that their toilet bowl cleaner, synthetic carpet, or pesticide is poisoning populations, but the precautionary principle can apply to our purchasing decisions.[30]

Walking along the Ohio River after its periodic floods, when the shoreline and sidewalk overflow not only with mud and driftwood, but with piles of plastic bottles, tires, Styrofoam coolers, and even the occasional Jacuzzi, I often wonder where, upstream from us, all this garbage originated, and what Louisville is sending down the river toward Paducah, Cairo, and eventually New Orleans and the Gulf of Mexico. We don't live in isolation, taking care of our own garbage. Rather, we all live downstream from someone, absorbing their waste, and upstream from someone else, fouling their waters.

What would Ezekiel say today about waters filled not simply with mud but with deadly toxins, and how would his words be received? As for Elijah, King Ahab was fond of calling him "my enemy" (1 Kgs. 21:20) and "troubler of Israel" (18:17). But as Elijah rightly pointed out, Israel's troubler was the one using his power unjustly. Elijah arrived in Jezreel too late to save Naboth. Since his words eventually caused Ahab to repent, one wonders what could have happened had Elijah arrived earlier, and what other tragic dramas the prophet did forestall. Like Elijah, people of faith concerned with justice bear responsibility to call both ourselves and our neighbors to account.

Questions for Thought and Discussion

1. What is your reaction to the Naboth story, and to the speeches of Isaiah and Ezekiel? Do you think they apply today? How?
2. What do you think are Christians' responsibilities to the poor? What forms do such responsibilities take?
3. Do you see people today as healthier or unhealthier than our parents and grandparents? What makes us healthier? What makes us unhealthier?
4. What are the results of chronically poor health (such as cancer, asthma, and allergies) for children?
5. What kinds of toxins do you think you encounter in daily life? Which ones are avoidable and how?
6. What does it mean to be a citizen and a responsible consumer? If you were to imagine a skill that you or your congregation possessed that could help change your community's pollution problems, what would it be?

Try This at Home

Take another inventory: what chemical products, from what sources and serving what purposes, do you find in your garage, basement, garden shed, cleaning closet, medicine cabinet, and vanity? What plastic products do you possess? Do you know how and where they were made? How are your electricity and gasoline produced? What are you unable to find out? Do some Internet searching, finding Web sites that rate the ecological impacts of some product lines.

Go to the EPA Web site, EJView (http://epamap14.epa.gov/ejmap/entry.html), type in your address, and learn about the sites nearby that must report toxic waste to the EPA. Scan your sources for information about local toxic pollutants. Visit some places you read or hear about.

We can learn how unnecessary many toxins are by reconsidering household cleaning products. Seek out "green" product lines such as Seventh Generation or Ecover. Better, find a Web site offering formulas for making your own cleaning products inexpensively, usually out of ingredients on hand. There are many, but the Toxics Use Reduction Institute (TURI) at the University of Massachusetts Lowell offers this one: http://www.turi.org/About/Library/TURI_Publications/Tip_Sheet_Series/Twelve_Home_Cleaning_Recipes. Try some out. What do you notice?

Our days are like the grass;
we flourish like a flower of the field;
when the wind goes over it, it is gone,
and its place shall know it no more.
But the merciful goodness of the Lord endures forever on the
    God-fearing,
and the righteousness of the Lord on children's children.
                                    —Psalm 103:15-17 (BCW)

As religious communities gradually awaken to the wisdom
of their traditional beliefs, they will also begin to recognize
that the environment is not only a political or a technological issue. For it is, in fact, primarily a religious and spiritual
issue. Any form of religiosity or spirituality that remains
disconnected from outward creation is ultimately also unin-
volved with the inward mystery of all things.
    —Orthodox Patriarch Bartholomew, Archbishop of Con-
        stantinople, "The Orthodox Church and the Environ-
        mental Crisis," in *Holy Ground: A Gathering of Voices on
        Caring for Creation*

Chapter 8

Our Children's Inheritance

The Unimaginable Future

Peculiar things happen in Genesis 15, the fourth time God tells Abraham that he will found a nation. God has him bring a menagerie of sacrificial animals—a heifer, a goat, a ram, a turtledove, and a pigeon. As the sun sets, Abraham falls asleep, and hears God saying:

> "Your offspring shall be aliens in a land that is not theirs, and shall be slaves there, and they shall be oppressed for four hundred years; but I will bring judgment on the nation that they serve, and afterward they shall come out with great possessions. . . . And they shall come back here in the fourth generation." (Gen. 15:13–14, 16)

Oddly, in verse 13 Abraham's descendants will leave Egypt after four hundred years. But in verse 16, they will leave in the fourth generation. This discrepancy has occasioned centuries of creative interpretation. Ancient rabbis speculated that if the descendants repented of their sins they would be returned in four generations, but if not, in four hundred years. Some modern scholars suggest the editor knew diverse traditions and didn't wish to choose one over another.

131

Without explaining away the discrepancy, we may notice that the difference between four generations and four centuries is the difference between the imaginable and the unimaginable future. Judging from our own great-grandparents' experience, we know that our children's children's children's world will be very different from ours. But what about four centuries? Do we even try to imagine life in the twenty-fifth century? Yet we look back to Abraham not from four generations, nor four centuries, but from nearly four thousand years. In this time his descendants—Jewish, Christian, and Muslim—have not simply traveled to Egypt and back, but have spread over the globe, several billion of us.

This passage reveals a double irony: on the one hand we can know the past, but we can no longer affect it. We can't change what ancestors did to create the world we know today. Yet by contrast, we can't know the future, but we affect it every day. Looking back at what we cannot change helps us see ourselves through future generations' eyes. We don't know them, but our successors will remember us and how we shaped their world.

Throughout this study we have explored many practices affecting future generations. In this chapter we will consider global climate change—the scientific discussion, the contemporary debate, and reasonable steps Christians might take. But first we'll examine a time in Judah's story that parallels the present.

Sour Grapes

The Ten Commandments speak of God as "punishing children for the iniquity of parents, to the third and fourth generation" and yet "showing steadfast love to the thousandth generation of those who love me and keep my commandments" (Exod. 20:5–6). The terms err on the side of generosity. Yet the passage still articulates an uncomfortable reality: children enjoy their ancestors' accomplishments, but also bear the brunt of their mistakes.

This was painfully apparent in the sixth century BCE when Jerusalem was destroyed by Babylon. Of earlier, foolish decisions that had led to up to this, exiles from Jerusalem said, "The parents have eaten sour grapes, and the children's teeth are set on edge" (Jer. 31:29). They had a right to complain. For years before the invasion, Jeremiah and other prophets had warned of disaster. But calls to change direction failed to inspire widespread response. Jeremiah observed:

> Their ears are closed,
>   they cannot listen.
> The word of the LORD is to them an object of scorn,
>   they take no pleasure in it.
>
> (Jer. 6:10)

Even other prophets found it easier to deny signs of trouble, and instead to curry short-term favor with hearers, especially the king and his supporters. Jeremiah said of them:

> From prophet to priest,
>   everyone deals falsely.
> They have treated the wound of my people carelessly,
>   saying, "Peace, peace,"
>   when there is no peace.
>
> (Jer. 6:13–14)

The problem with prophecy is that, until it is too late to act, hearers cannot be 100 percent certain which prophets to believe. It was easy to welcome claims of peace. Even after Babylon's first invasion in 597 BCE, when many were taken captive and the temple was plundered, some prophets still predicted that the crisis would soon end.

The young king Zedekiah sent officials to consult Jeremiah, hoping to hear something favorable (21:1–2). But Jeremiah counseled surrender. To illustrate his point, he wore an ox yoke, symbolic of forced servitude. But another prophet named Hananiah, who claimed that the exiles would soon return, underscored his own message by breaking Jeremiah's yoke (28:10). Jeremiah said he wished Hananiah might be right, but time would tell. Because

Jeremiah recommended surrender, he was accused of treason, and was beaten and imprisoned (37:11–16). Even the Babylonians seemed to think he was on their side (39:11–14; 40:1–6).

With the bitter exiles we can shake our heads over Jerusalem's disbelief. Jeremiah had been recommending policy changes for years. Early on, debate may have made sense. But as the threat became clearer, the debate became more heated, driven by reckless optimism that the unimaginable, the destruction of a temple, a city, and a kingdom that had stood four hundred years, could never occur.

In the church of Santa Maria del Carmine in Florence stands a gripping fifteenth-century fresco of Adam and Eve leaving the garden of Eden. It shows the pair mourning as they are driven forth by a red-clad angel. Eve is covering her breasts and genitals with her hands. Her mouth is open, her eyes closed, and her head uplifted. Viewers can almost hear her cry of remorse. Adam covers his face with both his hands, more ashamed of his deeds than his nakedness. The painting conveys intense regret. This story, ostensibly about exile from Eden, represented the anguish of those who lost the promised land.

Later generations in Babylon, like Adam and Eve, regretted having defied their limits. Modern history shows humans likewise defying limits and causing changes that reverberate across generations. Since the first atom bomb we have known that thoughtless human deeds could destroy us all. I remember my own childhood dread during air raid drills at school. I remember standing in the driveway at night during the Cuban missile crisis, looking southward and seeing nothing, yet still feeling dread. Who can forget the horrifying proliferation of the nuclear arms race and mutually assured destruction? Who now feels prepared to face another worldwide threat?

Yet this is exactly what nearly all the world's climatologists are predicting. Like Jeremiah's contemporaries, we are once again forced to decide which prophets to believe. Should we believe those warning of ecological disaster or those who say that nothing much is going on, and even that the real crisis is that some scientific radicals are crying wolf?[1]

Just as any wrong turn is more easily corrected in ten miles than fifty, the ecological issues raised so far in this study are better addressed sooner than later. But scientists warn that global climate change is far more time-sensitive than any other concern. We have a few years, not decades or centuries, to turn our course around.

When I began writing this book, I mentioned climate change on the first page. Church members objected that it was "too political" to mention first. They are right about its politicization in the United States, though not in the vast majority of other nations, which have generally accepted the scientific data. Unfortunately, much "climate change doubting" has been funded by industries fearing revenue loss from energy changes.[2] Yet as businesses and governments calculate the economic losses already piling up from global warming, minds are changing.[3] Many are becoming frustrated with a debate that has extended long past its reasonable time. It is like trying to convince people lingering in a burning building to save themselves—except that in this we can only be saved together. Assurances that things will be fine without significant action seem, like those voiced by Jeremiah's rivals, irrationally optimistic.

Carbon and Energy

Let's first review the science, starting with fundamentals. We all know that different solids and fluids have differing properties.[4] Gold, iron, calcium, carbon, and sulfur are all solid elements, but we can see, feel, and in some cases smell the differences among them. Similarly, though oxygen, nitrogen, argon, and carbon dioxide are all invisible gases, they too differ in behaviors. Most of the atmosphere is nitrogen (78 percent) and oxygen (20 percent). Argon comes next (1 percent). These three gases are simple: N_2, O_2, and Ar. Sunlight passes through them as if they were not there.

But the next most prevalent gas is carbon dioxide, CO_2. As a more complex molecule, it absorbs the sun's infrared light, trapping heat. This reality, which can be demonstrated by simple experiments, is called the "greenhouse" effect, and carbon dioxide is called a greenhouse gas. Other greenhouse gases are methane

(CH_4), water vapor (H_2O), nitrous oxide (N_2O), ozone (O_3), and a variety of chemically complex human-made gases such as CFCs and HFCs.

The more greenhouse gases there are in the lower atmosphere, or troposphere, the more sunlight is absorbed, warming the air. This is why Venus, whose atmosphere is more than 96 percent CO_2, has a surface air temperature of nearly 900 degrees F.[5] As long as the concentration of greenhouse gases in the earth's troposphere remains within a narrow range, they benefit us, warming the air to temperatures that support life.

Most life depends on plant photosynthesis. Energy from the sun interacts in plants with water and carbon dioxide to create carbohydrates such as glucose, with oxygen emitted as a byproduct ($6CO_2$ + $6H_2O$ + light energy $\rightarrow$ $C_6H_{12}O_6$ + $6O_2$). These organic carbon molecules store energy throughout the plant. When plants and those who have eaten plants respire, they reverse the photosynthetic process that stored the energy, releasing it for their own use.

The carbon in the earth's atmosphere is only a fraction of all the carbon on earth. The atmosphere contains 700 gigatons (Gtons, each a billion metric tons[6]) of carbon. The land surface contains about 500 Gtons in living beings (plants, animals) and 1,500 Gtons in dead carbon in the soils. The ocean contains even more: the living carbon tissues are only one Gton, but the oceans contain an additional 600 Gtons of dissolved organic matter and a whopping 38,000 Gtons of dissolved inorganic carbon.[7]

But the vast majority of carbon is found in sedimentary rocks such as limestone ($CaCO_3$): more than 1,000,000 Gtons. And sequestered with these rocks are the fossil fuels we mine for energy use: 5,000 Gtons. When these are burned for power, the chemical reaction releases carbon to the atmosphere, where it joins with oxygen to create CO_2. If we could burn all the fossil fuel that exists, we would add to the atmosphere all 5,000 Gtons, which is more than seven times more than is there currently, with a proportionate increase in atmospheric warming. It would use up all the oxygen, but first it would become too hot for survival.

We burn fossil fuels for the same reason we eat—to get the solar energy stored in carbon molecules. One gallon of gasoline consists of carbon created by ninety-eight tons of algae and plankton that sank to the ocean's bottom and were covered, pressurized, and cooked over millions of years.[8] "All the green the planet grows in four hundred years wouldn't quite produce the fossil fuels we burn in one," terrestrial ecologist Jeffrey Dukes estimates.[9] In the past century, enough fossil carbon has been released to increase the atmospheric ratio of CO_2 by more than 40 percent: from 260–280 parts per million (ppm) in preindustrial times to around 400 ppm today. During ice ages the CO_2 concentration was as low as 180–200 ppm.[10] In other words, CO_2 levels today are further from preindustrial levels than those were from ice-age levels. We've created a heat age.

A century ago scientists predicted that releasing carbon into the atmosphere would cause temperatures to rise.[11] Today climate scientists say that if our activities continue unchecked, the atmosphere's average temperature will rise by seven degrees Celsius (about 12 degrees Fahrenheit) by the end of this century.

The difference is huge. The last ice age was only five or six degrees cooler than now. Plants and animals, including ourselves, are adapted to the climate that exists and can't move or adapt fast enough to survive such dramatic change. Since adaptations differ among species that depend on one another, natural cycles are falling out of sync. Bees will be unavailable to pollinate vegetables, fruits, and other plants on which we depend. The berries on which some birds rely will not be available for them. The rains will not come when the seed is in the ground, as we saw in the summer of 2012 throughout the Midwest. And so on.

Seven degrees C is the *average* temperature rise, but the greatest rise, scientists say, is at the earth's poles. The measured rise in average global temperature is, so far, only 0.6 degrees Celsius, less than a tenth of what is anticipated. But already the northern ice cap is melting. Water sequestered as snow and ice in Antarctica and Greenland, as it melts, is already causing sea levels to rise. Glaciers and mountain snow that provide drinking water for billions of people are already receding, leading to drought.[12] Some places that were receiving rainfall are drier, and places already dry are becoming parched. In sub-Saharan Africa, for instance, the desert region is expanding, leading to famines. As cropland is lost and rain forests are destroyed for new fields, tens of thousands of species are disappearing every year.[13]

It helps to distinguish between climate and weather. Weather, as we know, changes day by day, and a weather forecast even a week in advance is inaccurate. So we may wonder how, if scientists can't predict weather for a week, they can predict climate for a century. It has to do with averages. When we toss a coin, we can only with fifty-percent accuracy predict how it will land. But if we toss a hundred coins, if we guess that about half will land heads up, we have a much greater chance of being right. Climate is the sum total of average weather trends over the course of a decade or more. That is why, though the trend in average temperature has been upward, with nine of the ten warmest years since 1880 having occurred since 2000, no one knows whether any particular year will follow that trend in every place.[14]

Until recently, scientists have hesitated to blame any particular weather event on climate change. But as droughts, floods, extreme highs and lows, and violent storms increase, this reluctance is changing. In a peer-reviewed study published in August 2012, NASA scientist James Hansen used statistical analysis to show that three recent climate events—the 2003 heat wave in Europe that killed tens of thousands, the 2010 heat wave in Russia and the Middle East that killed thousands, and the 2011 drought in Texas and Oklahoma—were caused by climate change.[15]

Some argue that sunspots are driving temperatures up. Sunspots do appear to be able to affect the climate. But if they were the driving force now, it would be the stratosphere, nearer to the sun, that would be warming. Instead the warming is near the surface, where we and all life are. Sunspot activity over the past thirty years has continued its usual variable cycle, with no trend upward or downward.[16]

Annual worldwide fossil fuel usage currently emits 7 Gtons of carbon. About 2 Gtons are absorbed by land and plants, and another 2 Gtons by the ocean. Three Gtons remain, warming the air. Over time both the land and the ocean are becoming less able to absorb these large amounts of carbon. In the meantime, the ocean's absorption of CO_2 is increasing its acidity, damaging marine life.[17] Climatologists say we cannot allow temperatures to rise past two degrees C, and that the oceans are acting as a heat sink, delaying this rise.[18] The effects will catch up more slowly, like the crash at the end of a long rush downhill.

In sum, scientists claim that: 1) climate change is occurring; 2) it is caused by greenhouse gases from human activity, particularly fossil fuel burning; and 3) as the temperature rises, the carefully balanced ecosystem on which we depend is endangered.[19]

It doesn't take scientific training to understand that as sea levels rise and temperatures change, not only plants and animals, but humans too must move. Given the resistance of nations to receiving refugees today and the violence that accompanies migration pressures, the interhuman struggle we face is large and unpredictable. A justice problem looms: wealthy nations and people have burned most of the fossil fuels, but the world's poor, who contributed least to the problems, are the most vulnerable. Finally, though, it will affect us all, rich and poor, ecologically aware and unaware, no matter whether we travel by jet or on foot.

On a lovely March day when the skies are clear and we welcome the blossoms of the dogwoods a month before their time, as many did in 2012, talk of danger seems farfetched. Unlike smog, greenhouse gases can't be seen or smelled. But the same invisibility was also operative in the 1970s when scientists discovered that the stratospheric ozone layer, which protects us from destructive ultraviolet rays, was being depleted by CFCs.[20] At that time the United States led the world in changing industrial practices, and the ozone layer has been healing.[21]

The Intergovernmental Panel on Climate Change

The Intergovernmental Panel on Climate Change (IPCC), comprised of thousands of researchers worldwide, was established in 1988 by the UN Environment Programme and the World Meteorological Organization. Its members review published, peer-reviewed scientific studies relevant to climate change and assess "the scientific, technical and socio-economic information relevant to understanding the scientific basis of risk of human-induced climate change, its potential impacts and options for adaptation and mitigation."[22]

Every few years the IPCC publishes reports summarizing scientific findings. These meticulously written reports, available on the Internet, include technical summaries and summaries for policymakers. Each successive report has raised the certainty level concerning human causes. The *Fifth Assessment Report*, appearing in September 2013, states that "human influence on the climate system is clear. This is evident from the increasing greenhouse gas concentrations in the atmosphere, positive radiative forcing, observed warming, and understanding of the climate system," and "it is *extremely likely* that human influence has been the dominant cause of the observed warming since the mid-20th century."[23]

Scientific consensus is based on accumulating evidence, verified, retested, and refined by differing teams of scientists. In the peer review process, a paper is typically read by at least three outside experts who assess its plausibility before publication in a reputable journal.[24] Thus a working scientist's standing depends on respectable research. There is little disagreement among such scientists about the causes and dangers of climate change. Yet much of the media, many politicians, and many in the American public still perceive a controversy, due to contrarian claims by nonscientists and by a few scientists who are paid to dispute the peer-reviewed science.

Climate skepticism comes in a variety of forms. Some claim that the climate is not changing. Others agree that it is changing, but deny that humans have caused it. Still others agree that humans are causing it but don't believe it will hurt us.[25] These three fundamentally different stances all share the same recommendation, "Do nothing." As evidence has mounted, some skeptics have moved from one of these positions to the next, showing that their claims are based on outcomes rather than facts. Yet "there simply isn't any wiggle room in the scientific literature on whether humankind is changing Earth's climate."[26]

The Rest of Us Nonspecialists

Wherever free speech is valued, anyone has the right to say anything and, just as in Jeremiah's day, listeners must use discernment to decide whom to believe. We may hope that some authority figure will pronounce truth and banish all debate, a voice from heaven, perhaps the angel Gabriel. The people in Jerusalem in the decade before its destruction could have used such clarity as well. But like us, all they got were circumstances and the prophets who interpreted them.

In our case, the prophets now warning of climate change include not only the vast majority of the scientific community, but a broad swath of religious leaders: the former Pope Benedict,[27] the Greek Orthodox Patriarch Bartholomew,[28] the Dalai Lama,[29] the former Archbishop of Canterbury Rowan Williams, along with Chief Rabbi Jonathan Sacks and leaders from every world faith community,[30] the World Council of Churches,[31] the National Council of Churches,[32] the National Association of Evangelicals,[33] the Presbyterian Church (U.S.A.),[34] and the Southern Baptist Convention.[35] World and national leaders are becoming less complacent: Defense Secretary Leon Panetta[36] and the Department of Defense[37] as well as leaders of the military branches;[38] British prime minister David Cameron;[39] more than a thousand U.S. mayors who, after the United States failed to ratify the Kyoto Protocol, committed their own cities to reduce emissions according to its goals;[40] the Republican governors of two large coastal states, Charlie Crist of Florida and Arnold Schwarzenegger of California[41]—the list of those becoming less willing to gamble goes on and on. Industry leaders are changing their minds as well. Some of the names on the EPA's Fortune 500 Green Power Partnership list are not surprising, such as Microsoft and Whole Foods, but second on the list after Intel is Kohl's Department Store, followed closely by Walmart and Lockheed.[42] Those of us who lack a scientific background can read the IPCC's summaries and other literature, assess the qualifications, claims, and logic of the writers, and decide for ourselves, not based on what we would like to believe, but on realistic appraisal.[43] If this issue is time-sensitive, we don't have time to be uninformed.

More importantly, we need not be convinced of climate change's threat to heed the warnings. Many or most of the changes recommended to mitigate climate change are also recommended to improve health, economy, security, and ecological stability in other ways.[44] For instance, we've heard repeatedly the ways money can be saved through electrical conservation. Walmart started saving $7 million per year simply by using CFLs in its store ceiling fan displays. This was so successful that the company developed LED lighting in refrigerators and saved another $3.8 million annually.[45] The same goes in transportation: Walmart, again, saved 28 to 30 percent in gas costs by updating their entire fleet for fuel efficiency between 2005 and 2010.[46] The state of Oregon discovered that for each megawatt of energy conserved, annual economic output increased by $2 billion, wages increased by nearly $700,000, business income increased by $125,000, and twenty-two jobs were created. By 2006 the state was saving 125 megawatts.[47]

Greenhouse gas conserving measures can also protect health by dramatically reducing air pollution, protecting waterways and their inhabitants, reducing both the mercury poisoning of sea-food and the fish kills resulting from pesticide runoff. Eating less beef, a measure that can substantially lower greenhouse gases, has been recommended for years by physicians. Walking or bicycling instead of driving has long been touted by both environmentalists and cardiologists. Conservation of fossil fuels also makes us more energy independent without the risky business of pumping "tar sand" oil in Canada and piping it across the continent, risking dangerous oil spills such as recent ones near the Great Salt Lake in Utah and in Mayflower, Arkansas, and more than a thousand others since 2010.[48] The list of convergences among ecological health, economic health, and human health goes on and on.

The precautionary principle, introduced in chapter 7 in rela-tion to toxic substances, applies to greenhouse gases as well. Pru-dence dictates approaching even local dangers with precautions in place. Even those who remain uncertain of climate change can approach this unknown frontier with caution. Few of us believe our own house will burn down, yet we still buy smoke alarms and fire insurance. We don't have to believe that global warming is a hundred percent probable, or ninety, or even fifty, to want to insure ourselves against it.

As Jeremiah demonstrated, it is reckless to convince ourselves that what we don't wish to happen won't happen. There is a crucial distinction to be made here between empty optimism and hope. Optimism believes that we needn't worry, nor act. If a problem exists someone else will solve it, just as they develop an iPhone app for every need. Hope, on the other hand, faces facts and fears. It doesn't leave the solutions to others but participates. Optimism is passive; hope is active.

Under the Kyoto Protocol, first adopted in 1997, industrialized countries agreed, as a starting point, to reduce their greenhouse gas emissions to a modest 5.2 percent below 1990 emission levels. The United States was one of the original signers, but alone failed to ratify it, citing lack of restrictions on developing nations, including China and India.[49] China, the United States, and India are the top three CO_2 emitting countries in the world. Yet per capita emissions tell a different story: 5.2 metric tons per person in China, 1.4 metric tons per person in India, and a whopping 17.5 tons per person in the United States, three times that of Chinese citizens and ten times the average Indian. Americans have extremely high expectations regarding the share of fossil fuel we are entitled to use. With five percent of the world's population, we account for nearly one-fourth of the world's total annual fossil fuel consumption.[50] We are the ones we are waiting for.

There is another way of looking at this: why should we expect other countries to take the lead at all? The United States has led the world in so many innovations: in democracy; in medicine; in inventions that saved lives and added pleasure, convenience, and creativity to the twentieth century. We were the first on the moon and the first to outlaw CFC's. Why shouldn't the world's richest nation lead now? One proposal for U.S. action suggests a unilateral approach:

> The first priority should be announcement of a coherent, effective mitigation strategy by the United States, matching or surpassing the climate leadership thus far exercised by the EU. . . . Initiatives by other major industrial economies to announce similar strategies in parallel would be welcome, but the initial development and announcement of a US strategy should not await coordination with others.[51]

As things stand, China, the country whose enormous population and increasing energy demand tempts Americans to object to regulating carbon, is becoming a clean energy leader, with a trillion-dollar market in green technology.[52] They are building what may become the world's largest wind farm, already six gigawatts, expected to triple by 2015, and are building enormous solar panel installations in the Gobi desert.[53] *New York Times* writer Thomas Friedman noted that "the view of China in the U.S. Congress—that China is going to try to leapfrog us by out-polluting us—is out of date. It's going to try to out-green us."[54] He quoted U.S. assistant secretary for policy and international affairs David Sandalow saying, "If they invest in twenty-first-century technologies and we invest in twentieth-century technologies, they'll win. If we both invest in twenty-first-century technologies, challenging each other, we'll all win."[55]

An Imaginable Future

Because some climate deniers have claimed that the costs of necessary changes are prohibitive, some people ask whether it is economically possible to forestall widespread ecological disaster. The IPCC cites three separate studies of the costs:

> Emission trajectories aiming to stabilize around 535 to 590 ppm of CO_2-equivalent had total costs that ranged from 0.2 to 2.5 percent of world economic output in 2030, and from small benefits to 4 percent loss in 2050. Stricter stabilization targets, from 445 to 535 ppm CO_2-equivalent, had costs of up to 3 percent in 2030 and up to 5 percent in 2050.[56]

Per capita U.S. GDP in 2011 was $48,442. So depending on whether we want to save the earth a little or a lot, the estimated price tag appears to be between $100 and $2400 per person per year, pennies or a few dollars per day. Given the political will, this can be done. Since we are already seeing hundred-billion-dollar pricetags for single events such as Hurricane Sandy, it is time to stop arguing that saving ourselves is too expensive.

Several years ago my husband and I began making changes in our hundred-year-old home. We changed the light bulbs, installed a programmable thermostat, insulated and weatherized the house, bought energy-star appliances, added power strips with off buttons, and installed two clotheslines, several ceiling fans, a tankless water heater, a small, energy efficient woodstove, a few replacement windows, and some blinds. These were not radical, high-tech, or costly changes. In five years we saved over $8,000, far more than we invested. We enjoy the comfort of a less drafty house, the convenience of better appliances, and the joy of a cheerful stove. Since our home is too shaded for solar panels, we can't get far past this point without changes in the energy infrastructure. Yet it took two years, not twenty, to move our energy use to a level that far exceeds standards the United States has yet to agree on.

The price of wind and solar power is dropping steadily, and in the long run these pay in free energy harvested directly from the sun and earth, rather than channeled through ancient algae and petroleum corporations. With fossil fuel prices continuing to rise, with oil spills and weather disasters ongoing, why not support research to raise the efficiency and continue lowering the cost of renewable energy?

In Jeremiah's time, the prophet and his foes alike assumed that God directed events, but they differed in their assumptions of what God would do. Jeremiah was more pragmatic than the deniers of his day. Happily, today we are disinclined to attribute disaster to God. Yet we still believe the universe has laws, and though a battle continues in the U.S. public over what these natural laws are, the issue is settled for the vast majority of scientists and leaders and for most of the world's other nations. By denying that Jerusalem could be destroyed, other prophets in Jeremiah's day were exercising brinksmanship. Jeremiah had fewer supporters than proponents of energy changes do, and no science on his side, but the public fight today is hardly less vicious than the one that had him imprisoned and nearly killed. It's time for churches to lead the public into calling the question. If necessary, we can let the petroleum industry and prevaricating politicians follow behind us.

This chapter began with God's invitation to Abraham to look to his descendants. Every generation faces new challenges as well as reasons to hope that we'll leave the world better for our children. When we ourselves were children, we were eager to grow to meet new responsibilities that signaled our maturity. Popular media does not favor mature behavior, since it can mean postponing self-indulgences their sponsors want to sell. Yet our lives don't belong to the media or their sponsors. Rather, our lives belong to our God, our family, our community, our selves. In an age in which the narrative all around us is the silliness of our political infighting and the frivolity and superficiality of our lifestyles, it doesn't take much to do better: in this case, to decide whether to heed the pandering prophets of peace or Jeremiah's responsible realism.

Questions for Thought and Discussion

1. Jeremiah lived through extraordinarily tumultuous times. What do you think kept him steady?
2. Have you ever been uncertain which "prophets" to believe? What is at stake when that happens? What is the safest action?
3. What has been your understanding of climate change? What have been your information sources? Do you think continued debate is worthwhile?
4. Which governmental, corporate, or religious leaders are taking climate change seriously? What are they doing?
5. What do you think churches need to do to address climate change? What do you believe families and communities should do?

Try This at Home

Go to the IPCC Web site and read some of the information provided there. What catches your eye? What concerns are raised? What do you learn?

Use Web searches to find out the energy policies and plans of other nations around the world. What is the tone of their discussions? What are they accomplishing?

Read *Cooler Smarter: Practical Steps for Low-Carbon Living*, by the Union of Concerned Scientists (Washington: Island Press, 2012). What practical actions are suggested? Can you reduce your household's greenhouse gas production? What other benefits can you see for doing this?

Write to your local and national politicians and your energy providers, telling them it is time to change our energy course.

"Enter through the narrow gate; for the gate is wide and the road is easy that leads to destruction, and there are many who take it. For the gate is narrow and the road is hard that leads to life, and there are few who find it."

—Matthew 7:13–14

We stand now where two roads diverge. But unlike the roads in Robert Frost's familiar poem, they are not equally fair. The road we have long been traveling is deceptively easy, a smooth superhighway on which we progress with great speed, but at its end lies disaster. The other fork of the road—the one less traveled by—offers our last, our only chance to reach a destination that assures the preservation of the earth.

—Rachel Carson, *Silent Spring*

Chapter 9

Living within Our Means

No Other World

I am writing while sitting by a large pond in September in southern Indiana. It is official: the first eight months of 2012 have been the hottest on record ever, and every county in our state, as well as far more than half the counties in the United States, have been declared drought disaster areas. The heat of June and July destroyed the crops when, encouraged by rising prices, farmers planted more corn than in the past seventy-five years.

I'm sitting near Henryville, a town raked by a tornado last March. Many houses and businesses are now being rebuilt, but the hillsides are still covered with uprooted trees. The only public school, which was completely destroyed, has been rebuilt and has opened. The weather began cooling in August, and rain fell in sudden violent downpours. The past several days have been too glorious for staying inside. They encourage forgetfulness.

A breeze from the south ripples the pond toward its shallow end. Except for this shimmering that breaks and refashions the shadows of trees on the far side, and the occasional splash of a fish, the day is still and sunlight sparkles like fireflies on the water. As the breeze picks up the firefly sparkles multiply on the pond's expanse and then taper off like a musical decrescendo. At this moment the crows are speaking—an hour ago, several hawks were whistling above. Fifteen minutes ago, five turkeys emerged from the woods and sauntered toward the pond, clucking and pecking the field as they walked.

This month the pond's banks are filled with thousands of yellow daisies. No one planted them and they weren't there last year. They sit precisely where I had planned to scatter wildflower seeds and never did. Across the way, a small ash tree has sprouted from the roots of a larger tree that died. I gaze at the ash with gratitude and sadness, knowing its prognosis is poor because of the invasive emerald borer that is killing most of our ashes.

A yellow butterfly lands on my foot and persists for most of the morning. When I move, it startles into flight. But then it returns, tickling with its proboscis. I did nothing to bring it into being or to invite its companionship, but its presence enriches my belief that, especially outdoors, good can cross human paths without any intent on our part. Other days I have seen other wonders—a heron standing vigil, a deer's silhouette on the hill, a family of geese, a dozen bats, a duck, a kingfisher, a pileated woodpecker.

Outdoors we learn not only the world of wounds of which Aldo Leopold spoke, but also the world of companionship to which the nonhuman world beckons us. It is hard to feel alone when you are surrounded by buzzing and chirping and splashing, when with every breeze a thousand daisies nod their heads at you, when the sun offers a light show in the pond, and would do so every day in every pond whether anyone is there to enjoy it or not.

E. O. Wilson calls it *biophilia*, love for nature, "the innate tendency to affiliate with life and lifelike processes."[1] He backs it up with science, saying that researchers have found that people of widely diverse cultures all tend to prefer similar settings: meadows dotted with trees with low, horizontal branches; a fruitful terrain populated by large animals; bodies of water in the background—much like the African savannah evolutionary scientists say we all come from. "Much of human nature was genetically encoded during the long stretches of time that our species lived in intimacy with the rest of the living world."[2] It's in our genes to find such places soothing. No wonder ancient writers described Eden this way as well.

There isn't another world like this within reach of human travel. No more frontiers can open up. The moon and Mars, everywhere else we could possibly escape to, we would have to artificially make our own reality, and it wouldn't be like this one, full of daisies we never planted. We can't discard this one. We have to mend it. It is not indestructible, but under favorable conditions it is, like all creatures including ourselves, resilient.

Micah's Vision

Our explorations of the Bible have taught us of both danger and resilience. These themes sit side by side in the book of Micah. Not much is known about the prophet except that he lived at the same time as Isaiah in the eighth century BCE in an outlying region of Judah. His town of Moresheth lay to Jerusalem's southwest, toward the Mediterranean coast, close to the Philistine city of Gath. If we knew its precise location we could drive there from Jerusalem in half an hour. But those twenty miles made all the difference.

In Micah's day, King Hezekiah of Jerusalem gambled dangerously. Trying to throw off foreign shackles, he withheld the tribute, or tax, being levied by the Assyrian empire. Every nation under tyrannical rule, from ancient Judah to modern Libya and Syria, faces such a gamble and weighs its options. But King Hezekiah lived inside the walls of Jerusalem, not out in the countryside where Micah was. In 701 BCE the Assyrians invaded Judah and, as 2 Kings 18:13 tells the story, captured all its fortified cities except Jerusalem before Hezekiah realized his grave mistake and reversed his position.

King Sennacherib's annals tell of the same incident from the emperor's viewpoint, describing his violent conquest of forty-six walled cities and countless villages of Judah. When archaeologists found his palace in Nineveh, they found the walls of a large room lined with a thirteen-paneled frieze depicting the gruesome battle against the largest of these cities, Lachish, not far from Moresheth.[3] This gripping frieze, now in the British Museum, depicts cruelty as appalling as any in our century, and a forlorn parade of refugees, adults and children, leaving the city and bowing before Sennacherib to beg for their lives.

It matters very much where Micah lived, and what he saw from there. We don't know at what point in the march of events he spoke, but we have to imagine that he had either already seen his town's destruction or recognized the danger it was in when he threatened that Jerusalem would suffer the same fate:

> Hear this, you rulers of the house of Jacob
>   and chiefs of the house of Israel,
> who abhor justice
>   and pervert all equity,
> who build Zion with blood
>   and Jerusalem with wrong!
> Its rulers give judgment for a bribe,
>   its priests teach for a price,
>   its prophets give oracles for money;
> yet they lean upon the Lord and say,
>   "Surely the Lord is with us!
>   No harm shall come upon us."
> Therefore because of you
>   Zion shall be plowed as a field;
> Jerusalem shall become a heap of ruins,
>   and the mountain of the house a wooded height.
>
> (Mic. 3:9–12)

Why do we care about Micah today? First, if we were to place Micah in relation to the contemporary world, he would not, like Isaiah who was evidently a royal advisor, have a bunker with the president. If he were a U.S. citizen at all, he would live in a region at risk. Or perhaps he would live completely outside the seat of power, Maldives perhaps, or along the encroaching Sahara of Africa, or among the floods of the Philippines. He would be one of those who cannot change our environmental course, but who will suffer the consequences of others' decisions.

Second, later generations in Jerusalem remembered Micah with gratitude. A century after his time, another group of prophets including Jeremiah, whom we discussed in chapter 8, were warning of new dangers approaching Jerusalem. When Jeremiah went to Solomon's temple next to the palace to speak, religious leaders seized and sought to execute him (Jer. 26:7). But palace officials heard Jeremiah's pleas and slowed the proceedings. Then some elders settled the case with these words:

> "Micah of Moresheth, who prophesied during the days of King Hezekiah of Judah, said to all the people of Judah: 'Thus says the LORD of hosts, Zion shall be plowed as a field; Jerusalem shall become a heap of ruins, and the mountain of the house a wooded height.' Did King Hezekiah of Judah and all Judah actually put him to death? Did he not fear the LORD and entreat the favor of the LORD, and did not the LORD change his mind about the disaster that he had pronounced against them? But we are about to bring great disaster on ourselves!" (Jer. 26:18–19)

Their ability to draw apt conclusions from Micah's story, and even to view his outraged forecast as a form of patriotism, helped save Jeremiah's life and Jerusalem's conscience.

Though Jerusalem didn't fall in Micah's lifetime, it did in Jeremiah's. Later, when the rebuilding nation sifted through its traditions for understanding, Micah's words became so central that the final verse concerning Jerusalem's destruction, Micah 3:12, was placed at the middle of the twelve minor prophets, to the exact verse. It was the pivot point.

But it wasn't the ending. By the time Micah's book reached the form we have it now, some words he probably didn't pen were attached to his own. These words are the third reason we should care. These words, far more familiar from the book of Isaiah, were appended immediately after Micah's dire threat, as if to heal the damage and reconcile the two prophets:

> In days to come
>   the mountain of the LORD's house
> will be established at the peak of the mountains,
>   and will be lifted up above the hills,
> and all the peoples will stream to it.
>   and many nations will come, and they will say,
> "Come, let us go up to the mountain of the LORD,
>   to the house of the God of Jacob,
> that we may be taught God's ways,
>   so we may walk in God's paths."
> From Zion will come teaching,
>   and the word of the LORD from Jerusalem.
> God will judge between many people,
>   and arbitrate between mighty nations far away.
> They will beat their swords into plowshares,
>   and their spears into pruning knives.
> Nation will not take up sword against nation,
>   and they will no longer train for war.
>   (Mic. 4:1–3, AT)

What an amazing word of hope and peace the two prophetic books share: a vision of a day when the world's nations seek to live according to the limits written into the earth's foundations by its creator, a day when economies devote themselves not to destruction but to tending and cultivating the earth that is our home, producing food instead of bombs. But Micah's version goes one step further. A final verse appears that is absent from Isaiah:

> They will all sit under their own vines and under their own fig trees,
>   and no one will disturb them;
>   for the mouth of the LORD of hosts has spoken.
>   (v. 4, AT)

Micah's unique vision shows everyone enjoying their own piece of Eden, secure and unafraid. What the book of Micah envisions for the future is a this-worldly hope, a time on this earth when peace allows all to prosper.

Biblical Eschatology

Toward the end of Isaiah a hope similar to that in Micah is found:

> See, I am creating a new heaven
>   and a new earth:
> past events will not be remembered,
>   and they will not come to mind.
> Be glad and rejoice for ever
>   in what I am creating,
> for I am creating Jerusalem a joy,
>   and her people a source of gladness.
> I will rejoice in Jerusalem
>   and be glad in my people,
> and there will not be heard in her again
>   a sound of weeping and crying.
> No more will babes live only a few days,
>   or the old fail to live out their days,
> for the hundred-year-old will die young,
>   and the one falling short of a hundred will seem cursed.
> They will build houses and live in them,
>   and they will plant vineyards and eat their fruit.
> They will not build for others to live in,
>   nor plant for others to eat.
> Like the days of a tree will be the days of my people,
>   and my chosen will fully enjoy the work of their hands.
> They will not labor in vain,
>   nor bear children for disaster,
> for they will be offspring blessed by the LORD,
>   they and their descendants as well.
>
>   (Isa. 65:17–23, AT)

Even though the prophet calls it a "new heaven and a new earth," once again we see here a this-worldly hope. This is eschatology, picturing future times. But unlike some violent popular eschatologies today, it is not a vision in which the faithful are raptured to heaven, leaving a ravaged earth behind. Rather, it's a world where people are born and live and die, but do so naturally and peacefully.

One of the Christian enemies of the environmental movement is the hope for escape from this world because, as the "Countdown" song goes, "Somewhere in outer space God has prepared a place for all those who trust him and obey": the hope that it doesn't matter what we do to this earth, since we will be gone. Ronald Reagan's controversial secretary of the interior from 1981 to 1983, James Watt, has frequently been quoted as saying during his term that the earth is "merely a temporary way station on the road to eternal life."[4]

Like Watt and the rest of us, Jesus himself was born into a tempestuous world that some, despairing, thought was better left behind. In fact, the first generation of apostles hoped that the world as they knew it would soon end. But Jesus had already cautioned against such fixations, instructing his disciples to live as if this world would go on, because no one, not even he, could predict its end (Mark 13:32). He said our job is to care faithfully for our home:

> "It is like a man going on a journey, when he leaves home and puts his slaves in charge, each with his work, and commands the doorkeeper to be on the watch. Therefore, keep awake—for you do not know when the master of the house will come, in the evening, or at midnight, or at cockcrow, or at dawn, or else he may find you asleep when he comes suddenly. And what I say to you I say to all: Keep awake." (Mark 13:34–37)

Jesus made clear that his followers should be at their post, doing their job, tending the house, not neglecting it, and certainly not destroying it.

The Bible contains many different visions of the future, most of them contrasting with dissatisfactions with present conditions. Christianity was born as a religion of eschatological hope. This hope has driven us from one generation to the next, founding hospitals and universities, defying slave trade and slavery, reforming governments, marching for civil rights, building affordable houses, and speaking out for those whose voices are not heard. Even when we temporarily forget, people of faith know well that we are called to defend "the least of these." What we haven't yet learned well is our relationship to the planet itself.

The Human Problem and the Church

This book began by observing that the world as we know it today is not the world as it always has been. Rather we've always seen changes, some of them revolutionary. Change—whether harmful or healthful—is inevitable. When some become convinced that business as usual has become indefensible, as William Wilberforce and others did in late eighteenth-century England, there is a period of struggle, as those who profit most from the entrenched system exert opposition. Sometimes, though, new ways emerge, and eventually become the norm.

Chapter 2 explored the biblical story of creation in Genesis 1–2. There we asked what it might mean that so much of creation preexisted us, what God's pleasure with creation might signify, and what we might understand by the powerful comments regarding human beings, that we were made in God's image and charged with dominion, and that we were given the vocation of serving and preserving the land.

If chapter 2 explored our connections, chapter 3 examined our disconnections: the story of the first couple in Eden, the violation of limitations set by God for them, their loss of paradise, and the first murder that resulted in alienation from the land itself. We discussed the flouting of ecological limits in the human quest for power, literally, in the form of electricity, and what this defiance has done to our air, water, and bodies. We explored what it means that we are intricately connected with the rest of creation's web.

In the remaining chapters we dealt with only a sampling of the specific ecological questions being raised. Chapter 4 explored consumerism and materialism. Greed has always been with us, but the abundance of goods and advertising has now multiplied its effect. We discussed consumerism's impact on our pocketbooks, our health, and the health of the planet whose resources are being mined, marketed, and discarded.

In chapters 5 and 6 we discussed problems with the American food system, which is increasingly being replicated around the globe. An industrial system has grown since the twentieth century that is neither feeding us well nor treating the land and its creatures with respect. We find a growing alternative in sustainable agriculture, consisting of appropriate land use, diversification, care for living creatures, and technologies that maintain the health of soil, water, and life.

In chapter 7 we explored the problems of environmental justice, particularly in the form of toxic waste generated close to poor communities. Finally, in chapter 8 we discussed the urgent problem of global climate change, exploring both the science and the politics of the debate, finding precedent in Scripture to guide our approach.

This book is by no means comprehensive. Rather I hope that exploring some issues alongside Scripture will inspire further seeking. Most of us already recognize the ecological concerns that were raised. The challenges are, first, to connect the dots between our love for God and humans and our love for creation and, second, to let this love inform our actions.

United Church of Christ minister Peter Sawtell describes an approach he takes with church groups. He begins with newsprint and markers and invites the group to name ecological issues they care about. He says they quickly generate a long list. As the brainstorming continues, they begin to draw interconnections between related concerns, such as asthma, toxic waste, and urban poverty, or pesticide use, farm worker health, and farm sewage. When the paper fills up, they stare at the list for a few moments, soaking it in. Then he says:

All the issues on the newsprint are just symptoms of one central, essential problem: humans are living out of whack with the Earth. In our modern industrial world, we are living in a distorted, dysfunctional relationship with the rest of creation. "We don't have environmental problems," I say. "We have a human problem."[5]

He goes on to observe that though there is work to be done on energy efficiency and pollution control, the most important work is to change our beliefs, "to claim a new way of living in relationship with the entire Earth community."[6] If the ecological crisis is a human problem, as he says, "if we're struggling with a warped notion of humanity's place and purpose in creation, then faith communities have vast expertise in dealing with that problem."[7]

Since ancient times, faith communities have reached past failure for renewed relationships with humanity and with God. Ecological questions constitute another chapter in this quest. As our readings of Scripture have shown, concern for the nonhuman world is not by any means new. But as humans have become increasingly divorced from the earth, and as our destructive capabilities have multiplied, this concern is more urgent than ever. It is time to be asking ourselves what humans are here for, and what our relationships say about us.

Making Plans

Inaction breeds despair. We can't get anywhere by sitting like a ship in the harbor. If we have not done so already, it's time to set out. We can begin by making sustainable, appropriate plans, tailored to our own capabilities and resources, shifting our intentions from making a good *living* to making a good *life*. They are not the same. Making a good life doesn't rule out financial success or security, but it does alter our relationship to money, things, and our own life's work.

Some of us hear in the environmental crisis a call to full-time action. There are indeed more and more opportunities—many of them entrepreneurial—for inventors, small-business people, lawyers, builders, teachers, doctors, scientists, farmers, preachers, politicians, activists, social workers, writers, actors—people of every talent and training—to find a full-time niche in the industry of mending the human relationship to the earth. Some see an immediate convergence between their time and opportunities and the world's needs.

The rest of us, working in other sectors, also have many opportunities in our homes, churches, and communities. The point is not where we are now but what direction we are heading. We never know when a tailwind will push us. It's a matter of priorities, a matter of joy, a matter of breaking away from broken systems that use us, into more vivid, vital lives.

I am no expert on planning, but I can say what works for me. Here are some basics:

1. *Include creation in your prayers every day*, both in gratitude and concern.
2. *Learn more.* The notes and the "For Further Reading" section in this book offer many starting places. In most communities forums, clubs, and organizations can be found where more can be learned. Many states have chapters of Interfaith Power and Light, a faith-based environmental organization. Environmental blogs can keep us informed.
3. *Set goals for your home life, work life, church life, and community life.* For instance: 1) Living in gratitude for, and communion with, the web of creation; 2) Rejecting consumerism and embracing simplicity; 3) Sifting every decision through the screen of these values of gratitude, communion, and simplicity.
4. *Begin to make and follow an action plan*, just as you would for a major work or family project. Break it down into categories and steps. Make a checklist. Review and revise your plan periodically, every month or three months.
5. *Create new habits that become second-nature.* These can't be done all at once. What worked for me was to plan one significant household change for every month for several

years. For resources for a churchwide effort, see http://
www.hoosieripl.org/task-of-the-month.
6. *Communicate your values to others.* Teach children and
   young people; take opportunities that arise in conversations with friends and acquaintances. Start a "green
   team" at church. Start a book group. Approach colleagues
   at work about changing institutional practices. Call and
   write government officials and manufacturers of products
   you buy. Write letters to the editor. Write a book.
7. *If you see a larger opportunity, take it.*

The need to change the human course has never been greater,
nor more urgent. The means to change the world has never been
greater either. The question is the will to do so. Though each
of us can only control our own actions, we can influence a great
many others.

Jesus was a master of the one-minute story. He once told this
one-sentence parable: "The kingdom of heaven is like a merchant
in search of fine pearls; on finding one pearl of great value, he went
and sold all that he had and bought it" (Matt. 13:45–46). We can
imagine that such an experienced merchant would not be dazzled
by any second-class jewel. So we can appreciate his realization of
having found, and almost having in hand, not just *a* good pearl, but
the one worth giving up the search for any others. Had he been
a less discriminating connoisseur, selling everything he owned to
get this pearl might have been reckless. But Jesus commends him
for knowing what is priceless when he sees it. In Jesus' estimation,
the kingdom of heaven is the one thing worth all else, the one
thing for which a rational person might give everything. Jesus also
made clear that this kingdom of heaven, this realm of God's good
pleasure, is not somewhere else in the sky, nor far across the sea,
but here among us (Luke 17:21). He demonstrated his commitment to this reign of God on earth exactly as the merchant had
done, by giving all he possessed, life itself, in order to redeem it.

Today we find ourselves contemplating a jewel resembling a
sapphire more than a pearl, the exquisite blue earth that astronauts have photographed for us. We see in full view, from above,

the habitat that God provided all creatures so long ago. From a distance it may appear peaceful, and yet we know how troubled it is. If we are as shrewd as that merchant, as wise as Jesus himself, we will not waste our lives calculating whether another jewel will come along later. This is the one in which we will invest ourselves, and the choice will be life-changing.

The central road through Brown County State Park in Indiana travels along a ridge overlooking what seems like the whole rest of the state, if not the world. You can drive a mile or two seeing only dense, high forest enclosing all sides, and then suddenly encounter an opening in the trees that offers a distant view of the hill skidding down to valleys, with layers of green hillsides on the far horizon, often decked in mist. These vistas come upon you like momentary clarity, and then they are past.

Walking a trail around a lake there a couple of weekends ago, just as the leaves were edging toward crimson, I saw a young mother directing her daughter's attention upward, to gaze at a brilliant maple tree that stood behind me. The little girl looked upward and gasped in awe. "It's a *miracle!*" she announced, with the solemnity of one who knows a miracle when she sees one. I had to turn around and see the tree again, through her eyes. And indeed it was—a miracle.

Questions for Thought and Discussion

1. What ambivalences haunt you as you consider the state of the physical world? To what specific places or natural things do you find yourself attached? What fears or worries do you have?

2. Can a person such as Micah be both patriotic and critical of the actions of a government, its leaders, or its citizens? What are constructive ways to express differences? Under some circumstances, can silence be less than faithful?

3. Do you know someone who is working full time to help address ecological issues? What do they do? What do they say about how they arrived at vocational decisions? How do they feel about their work?

4. What talents, interests, skills, or passions do you bring to mending the earth? Whom would you like to invite to work with you?

5. What specific issues matter the most to you? Do you already envision some ways to address them? If you have already begun to address them, what have you learned?

Try This at Home

Look at the list of seven actions in the section called "Making Plans." How would you flesh out this list for yourself? What is your action plan? How will you involve children, family, and friends?

If you read this book with friends or church members you might look together at the "For Further Reading" section and consider another book to read together. If you read this book alone, you are now qualified to lead a group in reading this one together. Please consider doing so.

The first action suggestion in chapter 1 was, "For the next week, as you read the Bible or hear Scripture read in church, pay attention to what is said about creation, the earth, and its creatures. Try your hand at a little writing. It may be a poem, a prayer, or simply a list. Try putting on paper two things: first, the gifts of life that you cherish most, and second, what concerns you most about the state of the world. If you have children, you might consider inviting them to express their joys and concerns as well." Try this again now, and next week, and the next.

Key Passages

One primary passage for each chapter is listed first in bold, and other passages are listed in the order in which they appear in the chapter.

Chapter 1: **Isaiah 43:16–19;** Acts 9:1–16

Chapter 2: **Genesis 1:1–2:3, 15;** Psalm 104; Isaiah 43:19–21

Chapter 3: **Genesis 3:1–4:16;** Hosea 4:1–3; Isaiah 24:4–6

Chapter 4: **Isaiah 2:1–21;** Psalm 10:2–4; Proverbs 16:18–19, 30:8–9

Chapter 5: **Exodus 16:13–26;** Leviticus 25:1–28; 19:9–10; Exodus 23:10–11

Chapter 6: **Genesis 1:29–30;** 9:2–3; Isaiah 11:6–9; Leviticus 11:1–30; 17:3–4, 10–14; 2 Samuel 12:1–4; Proverbs 27:23–27

Chapter 7: **1 Kings 21:1–24;** Isaiah 5:1–8; 10:1–2; Ezekiel 34:17–23

Chapter 8: **Genesis 15:13–16;** Jeremiah 6:10–14; 28:1–17

Chapter 9: **Micah 3:9–4:5;** Isaiah 65:17–23; Mark 13:34–37; Matthew 13:45–46

Genesis 1:1–2:3

This litany calls for five readers, labeled A through E.

A: In the beginning when God created the heavens and the earth, the earth was a formless void and darkness covered the face of the deep, while a wind from God swept over the face of the waters.

B: Then God said, "Let there be light";

A: and there was light.

C: And God saw that the light was good;

D: and God separated the light from the darkness.

E: God called the light Day, and the darkness God called Night.

All: And there was evening and there was morning, the first day.

B: And God said, "Let there be a dome in the midst of the waters, and let it separate the waters from the waters."

D: So God made the dome and separated the waters that were under the dome from the waters that were above the dome.

A: And it was so.

E: God called the dome Sky.

All: And there was evening and there was morning, the second day.

B: And God said, "Let the waters under the sky be gathered together into one place, and let the dry land appear."

A: And it was so.

E: God called the dry land Earth, and the waters that were gathered together God called Seas.

C: And God saw that it was good.

B: Then God said, "Let the earth put forth vegetation: plants yielding seed, and fruit trees of every kind on earth that bear fruit with the seed in it."

A: And it was so. The earth brought forth vegetation: plants yielding seed of every kind, and trees of every kind bearing fruit with the seed in it.

C: And God saw that it was good.

All: And there was evening and there was morning, the third day.

B: And God said, "Let there be lights in the dome of the sky to separate the day from the night; and let them be for signs and for seasons and for days and years, and let them be lights in the dome of the sky to give light upon the earth."

A: And it was so.

D: God made the two great lights—the greater light to rule the day and the lesser light to rule the night—and the stars. God set them in the dome of the sky to give light upon the earth, to rule over the day and over the night, and to separate the light from the darkness.

C: And God saw that it was good.

All: And there was evening and there was morning, the fourth day.

B: And God said, "Let the waters bring forth swarms of living creatures, and let birds fly above the earth across the dome of the sky."

D: So God created the great sea monsters and every living creature that moves, of every kind, with which the waters swarm, and every winged bird of every kind.

C: And God saw that it was good.

B: God blessed them, saying, "Be fruitful and multiply and fill the waters in the seas, and let birds multiply on the earth."

All: And there was evening and there was morning, the fifth day.

B: And God said, "Let the earth bring forth living creatures of every kind: cattle and creeping things and wild animals of the earth of every kind."

A: And it was so.

D: God made the wild animals of the earth of every kind, and the cattle of every kind, and everything that creeps upon the ground of every kind.

C: And God saw that it was good.

B: Then God said, "Let us make humankind in our image, according to our likeness; and let them have dominion over the fish of the sea, and over the birds of the air, and over the cattle, and over all the wild animals of the earth, and over every creeping thing that creeps upon the earth."

D: So God created humankind in God's image, in the image of God they were created; male and female God created them.

B: God blessed them, and God said to them, "Be fruitful and multiply, and fill the earth and subdue it; and have dominion over the fish of the sea and over the birds of the air and over every living thing that moves upon the earth." God said, "See, I have given you every plant yielding seed that is upon the face of all the earth, and every tree with seed in its fruit; you shall have them for food. And to every beast of the earth, and to every bird of the air, and to everything that creeps on the earth, everything that has the breath of life, I have given every green plant for food."

A: And it was so.

C: God saw everything that God had made, and indeed, it was very good.

All: And there was evening and there was morning, the sixth day.

A: Thus the heavens and the earth were finished, and all their multitude. And on the seventh day God finished this work, and rested on the seventh day from all God's work. So God blessed the seventh day and hallowed it, because on it God rested from all God's work in creation.

Notes

Chapter 1: The Problem of Change, Then and Now

1. E. O. Wilson, *The Creation: An Appeal to Save Life on Earth* (New York: Norton & Co., 2006), 5.
2. Ibid., 27.
3. Wendell Berry, *The Citizenship Papers: Essays* (Washington, DC: Shoemaker and Hoard, 2003), 135.

Chapter 2: Humans and Creation

1. See David S. Cunningham, "The Way of All Flesh: Rethinking the *Imago Dei*," in *Creaturely Theology: On God, Humans, and Other Animals*, ed. Celia Deane-Drummond and David Clough (London: SCM Press, 2009), 100–117.
2. Ruth Page, *God and the Web of Creation* (London: SCM Press, 1996), 118.
3. Ibid., 119.
4. Daniel K. Miller, "Responsible Relationship: *Imago Dei* and the Moral Distinction between Humans and Other Animals," *International Journal of Systematic Theology* 13, no. 3 (2011): 323–39. Drawing on Emil Brunner and Karl Barth, he notes that "we cannot speak definitively about the ways other creatures relate to God because we simply do not know what it is like to be another creature in relation to God. . . . Whether and in what way God addresses other animals is shrouded in mystery" (331).
5. William P. Brown observes, "The *imago* dimension of human creation in Genesis 1 encompasses all the cognitive, emotive, and cultural aspects that constitute a distinctly human identity" (*The Seven Pillars of Creation: The Bible, Science, and the Ecology of Wonder* [New York: Oxford University Press, 2010], 65). He goes on to quote J. Wentzel van Huyssteen, who says, "No single trait or capacity like intelligence or rationality should ever be taken

as the definitive word on human uniqueness" (*Alone in the World? Human Uniqueness in Science and Theology* [Grand Rapids: Eerdmans, 2006], 106).

6. Indeed, scriptural writers imagine God in the form of many animals, such as eagles (Exod. 19:4; Deut. 32:11–12), hovering birds (Isa. 31:5); lions (Isa. 31:5; 38:13; Jer. 25:38; 49:19; 50:44; Lam. 3:10; Hos. 5:14; 11:10; 13:7), leopards (Hos. 13:7), and bears (Lam. 3:10; Hos. 13:8). They also speak of the cosmos reflecting God's glory (Ps. 8:1; 19:1; 50:6; Rom. 1:19–20).

7. Lynn Townsend White Jr., "The Historical Roots of Our Ecological Crisis" Available at http://www.uvm.edu/~gflomenh/ENV-NGO-PA395/articles/Lynn-White.pdf. Originally published in *Science* 155 (March 10, 1967):1203–7.

8. The NRSV and NIV correctly follow the ancient Syriac translation and the opinions of a large number of scholars in restoring the three-letter word meaning "wild animals" to v. 26 (as in v. 25), rather than reading "all the earth," which abruptly interrupts the list of species.

9. Steven Mithen's fascinating study, *After the Ice: A Global Human History 20,000–5000 BC* (Cambridge, MA: Harvard University Press, 2006), portrays this history. According to Mithen, much of the development of domestic agriculture took place in and around what would become Canaan and, later, Israel and Judah.

10. David J. Bryant, "*Imago Dei*, Imagination, and Ecological Responsibility, *Theology Today* 57, no. 1 (2000): 35–50.

11. See Ellen F. Davis, *Scripture, Culture, and Agriculture: An Agrarian Reading of the Bible* (Cambridge, MA: Cambridge University Press, 2009), 29–30.

12. Wendell Berry, "Nature as Measure," in *Bringing it to the Table: On Farming and Food* (Berkeley, CA: Counterpoint, 2009), 3–4.

13. Lewis Thomas, *The Lives of a Cell: Notes of a Biology Watcher* (New York: Penguin Books, 1974), 145.

Chapter 3: Leaving the Garden

1. Thomas Berry, *The Sacred Universe: Earth, Spirituality, and Religion in the Twenty-First Century* (New York: Columbia University Press, 2009), 44.

2. Theodore Hiebert, "The Human Vocation: Origins and Transformations in Christian Traditions," in *Christianity and Ecology: Seeking the Well-Being of Earth and Humans*, ed. Dieter T. Hessel and Rosemary Radford Ruether (Cambridge, MA: Harvard University Center for the Study of World Religions, 2000), 139.

3. Ellen Davis, "Becoming Human: Biblical Interpretation and Ecological Responsibility," https://www.vts.edu/ftpimages/95/misc/misc_53462.pdf.

4. Brigitte Kahl, "Fratricide and Ecocide: Rereading Genesis 2–4," in *Earth Habitat: Eco-Injustice and the Church's Response*, ed. Dieter T. Hessel and Larry Rasmussen (Minneapolis: Fortress Press, 2001), 57.

5. http://www.statemaster.com/graph/ene_coa_con_percap-energy-coal
-consumption-per-capita.

6. "The Hidden Costs of Energy: Unpriced Consequences of Energy Production
and Use," http://books.nap.edu/openbook.php?record_id=12794&page=R1.

7. This externalization of costs is the reason behind proposals of carbon
taxes. Like Pigovian taxes on cigarettes and alcohol, the intentions are to
discourage excessive use and recoup societal costs. A growing number of
countries worldwide have imposed carbon taxes. Some advocates propose
that such taxes could replace other taxes while still generating revenue.
See "Where Carbon Is Taxed," http://www.carbontax.org/progress/where
-carbon-is-taxed/.

8. Pat Watkins, "Building Creation on a Firm Foundation," in *Love God, Heal
Earth*, ed. Sally G. Bingham (Pittsburgh: St. Lynn's Press, 2009), 24.

9. Wes Jackson, *Becoming Native to This Place* (Washington, DC: Counterpoint, 1996), 57.

10. Ibid., 2, 73–74.

11. Virgil, *The Georgics*, trans. Smith Palmer Bovie (Chicago: University of
Chicago Press, 1966), 5, quoted in Jackson, *Becoming Native*, 73.

12. Jackson, *Becoming Native*, 84.

13. Ibid., 26.

14. Davis, "Becoming Human," 9.

15. Jackson, *Becoming Native*, 75.

16. Charles Darwin, *The Annotated Origin: A Facsimile of the First Edition of On
the Origin of Species* (Cambridge, MA: Belknap Press, 2009), 489.

17. Richard Cartwright Austin, *Baptized into Wilderness: A Christian Perspective
on John Muir* (Atlanta: John Knox Press, 1987), 24-25.

18. Ruth Page, *God and the Web of Creation* (London: SCM Press, 1996), xii–xiii.

19. Davis, "Becoming Human," 5.

20. I tell this story in "Persistent Vegetative States: People as Plants and Plants as
People in Isaiah," in *The Desert Will Bloom: Poetic Visions of Isaiah*, ed. J. Everson
and P. Kim (Atlanta: Society of Biblical Literature Press, 2009), 17–34.

21. Hannah Holmes, *Suburban Safari: A Year on the Lawn* (New York:
Bloomsbury Publishing, 2005).

22. Stacey O'Brien, *Wesley the Owl: The Remarkable Love Story of an Owl and His
Girl* (New York: Free Press, 2009).

23. Ursula Goodenough, *The Sacred Depths of Nature* (Oxford University Press,
2000).

Chapter 4: Commerce and Contentment

1. R. R. Reno, "Pride and Idolatry," *Interpretation* 167 (April 2006), 166–78
(172–73).

2. Ibid., 173.

3. Ibid., 180.

4. Patrick McNamara, *The Neuroscience of Religious Experience* (Cambridge, MA: Cambridge University Press, 2009), 147.

5. Augustine, *Confessions of Saint Augustine* 1.1.

6. John De Graaf, David Wann, and Thomas H. Naylor, *Affluenza: The All-Consuming Epidemic*, 2nd ed. (San Francisco: Berrett-Koehler Publishers, 2005), 115.

7. This is the theme of Barry Schwartz, *The Paradox of Choice: Why More Is Less* (New York: Harper Perennial, 2004).

8. Bill McKibben, *Deep Economy: The Weath of Communities and the Durable Future* (New York: Times Books, 2007), 34–35.

9. De Graaf et al. compare this kind of shopping to other addictions, such as gambling (*Affluenza*, 112–13).

10. See, for instance, John Helliwell et al., eds., "World Happiness Report," http://www.documentcloud.org/documents/330305-happiness.html#document/p4.

11. Ibid.; Emily Alpert, "Happiness Tops in Denmark, Lowest in Togo, Study Says," (April 2, 2012), http://latimesblogs.latimes.com/world_now/2012/04/happiness-world-bhutan-meeting-denmark.html.

12. Happy Planet Index, www.happyplanetindex.org.

13. Thorstein Veblen, *The Theory of the Leisure Class: An Economic Study of Institutions* (Norwood, MA: Norwood Press, 1899), 31.

14. This history is detailed by Jeffrey Kaplan in "The Gospel of Consumption," *Orion Magazine*, May–June 2008 (http://www.orionmagazine.org/index.php/articles/article/2962/).

15. Quoted in Benjamin Kline Hunnicutt, "The End of Shorter Work Hours," 25 (1984), 373-404, http://www.uiowa.edu/~lsa/bkh/lla/eosh.htm.

16. De Graaf et al., *Affluenza*, 38.

17. Ibid., 77.

18. Doris Janzen Longacre, *Living More with Less*, 30th anniversary ed. (Scottdale, PA: Herald Press, 2010).

19. Duane Elgin, *Voluntary Simplicity: Toward a Way of Life That Is Outwardly Simple, Inwardly Rich* (New York: William Morrow, 1981).

20. John F. Kavanaugh, *Following Christ in a Consumer Society*, 25th anniversary ed. (Maryknoll, NY: Orbis Books, 2006).

21. Kaplan, "Gospel of Consumption."

22. Maryland's Genuine Progress Indicator (http://www.green.maryland.gov/mdgpi/).

23. Annie Leonard, *The Story of Stuff: How Our Obsession with Stuff Is Trashing the Planet, Our Communities, and Our Health—and a Vision for Change* (New York: Free Press, 2010), ix.

24. Elizabeth J. Canham, "Simplicity," in *Heart Whispers: Benedictine Wisdom for Today* (Nashville: Upper Room Books, 1999), 63.

25. Ibid., 67.

Chapter 5: Food for Life

1. "The State of Food: A Snapshot of Food Access in Louisville," 3. Online: http://www.louisvilleky.gov/NR/rdonlyres/E8C0D055-E234-489D-A592 -7792E323D106/0/StateofFoodFINAL.pdf. Accessed 23 June 2012.
2. Ibid., 4, 9, citing K. Morland, S. Wing, and A. Diez Roux, "The Contextual Effect of the Local Food Environment on Residents' Diets: The Atherosclerosis Risk in Communities Study," *American Journal of Public Health* 92/11 (Nov. 2002): 1761–67.
3. http://www.myfoodpoisoninglawyer.com/2011/04/simon-luke-prosecutes -salmonella-egg-claims-nationwide-video-here/. According to the CDC, "The decrepit conditions in these henhouses reflect the fact that companies know that FDA inspections are so rare . . . that there is no urgency to fix their buildings and their operations to assure compliance with FDA statutes and regulations" ("FDA Reports Numerous Violations at Egg Farms," CNN, August 31, 2010, http://www.cnn.com/2010/HEALTH/08/30/eggs .salmonella/index.html). For commentary on the subsequent congressional fight over regulations, see Michael Pollan and Eric Schlosser, "A Stale Food Fight," *New York Times*, Nov 29, 2010, http://michaelpollan.com/ articles-archive/a-stale-food-fight/.
4. "Bottled Water: Pure Drink or Pure Hype?" Natural Resources Defense Council, http://www.nrdc.org/water/drinking/bw/exesum.asp. See also "Bottled Water Demand May Be Declining," Worldwatch Institute: http:// www.worldwatch.org/node/5878.
5. See, for instance, James Pritchard, *The Ancient Near East: Supplementary Texts and Pictures Relating to the Old Testament* (Princeton: Princeton University Press, 1969), 37 plate 122; 42 plates 142 and 143.
6. Ellen Davis, *Scripture, Culture, and Agriculture: An Agrarian Reading of the Bible* (Cambridge, MA: Cambridge University Press, 2009), 68.
7. Ibid., 75–77.
8. Bill McKibben, *Deep Economy: The Wealth of Communities and the Durable Future* (New York: Times Books, 2007), 52.
9. Michael Pollan, *The Omnivore's Dilemma: A History of Four Meals* (New York: Penguin, 2007), 34.
10. Joel Salatin, owner of Polyface Farm in Virginia's Shenandoah Valley, offers a well-known example of closing the ecological loop as he grows grass-fed livestock, poultry, and eggs on land that the animals fertilize and the humans manage. He boasts that his family has not bought a sack of fertilizer in fifty years (http://www.polyfacefarms.com/principles/).
11. Pollan, *Omnivore's Dilemma*, 68.
12. Ironically, case studies have shown that "small farms almost always produce far more agricultural output per unit area than larger farms," both in the

United States and around the world (Peter Rosset, "Small Is Bountiful," *Ecologist* 29.8 [1999]: 452–56).

13. Pollan, *Omnivore's Dilemma*, 63. For another discussion detailing similar issues, which uses the 2009 dairy crisis as a case study, see "Taking on Corporate Power in the Food Supply," a March 2011 fact sheet assembled by Food and Water Watch, http://foodandwaterwatch.org/factsheet/taking-on-corporate-power-in-the-food-supply/.

14. Ben Lilliston, "Who's Benefitting from Higher Farm Prices," *Institute for Agriculture and Trade Policy*, April 13, 2011, http://www.iatp.org/blog/201104/whos-benefitting-from-higher-farm-prices.

15. Ben Lilliston, "What Does the Occupation of Wall Street Have to Do with Agriculture?" *Institute for Agriculture and Trade Policy*, Sept. 30, 2011, http://www.iatp.org/blog/201109/what-does-the-occupation-of-wall-street-have-to-do-with-agriculture. See also this more detailed report: "Commodities Market Speculation: The Risk to Food Security and Agriculture," *Institute for Agriculture and Trade Policy*, 2008, http://www.iatp.org/files/451_2_104414.pdf.

16. David Banker, "Production Shifting to Very Large Family Farms," *Amber Waves* (June, 2005), http://webarchives.cdlib.org/sw1vh5dg3r/http://www.ers.usda.gov/AmberWaves/June05/Findings/ProductionShifting.htm.

17. Lilliston, "Who's Benefitting."

18. See for instance the Action Aid International USA report "Biofueling Hunger: How U.S. Corn Ethanol Policy Drives Up Food Prices in Mexico," May 2012, http://www.actionaid.org/publications/biofueling-hunger-how-us-corn-ethanol-policy-drives-food-prices-mexico. Food prices in Mexico have risen more than 50 percent in the past five years, resulting in more than half of all Mexicans suffering some period of food insecurity in 2011. Rising food prices have increased by 44 million the number of people worldwide living below the extreme poverty line.

19. See Alexander E. Farrell, Richard J. Plevin, Brian T. Turner, Andrew D. Jones, Michael O'Hare, and Daniel M. Kammen, "Ethanol Can Contribute to Energy and Environmental Goals," *Science* 506.311 (27 January 2006), http://rael.berkeley.edu/ebamm/FarrellEthanolScience012706.pdf. Their findings show that the only kind of ethanol with potential to save substantially in fossil fuel and its pollution is cellulosic, that is, what is produced from wood, grass, or the inedible parts of grass. Corn ethanol, by contrast, uses a substantial amount of coal and natural gas.

20. Pollan, "How to Feed the World," *Newsweek*, May 19, 2008. http://michaelpollan.com/articles-archive/how-to-feed-the-world/.

21. Pollan, *Omnivore's Dilemma*, 63. For stories of such effects on farmers in India, see Vandana Shiva, *Stolen Harvest: The Hijacking of the Global Food Supply* (Cambridge, MA: South End Press, 2000). Shiva, an Indian physicist and environmental activist, has contributed to the fields of biodiversity, biotechnology, bioethics, and genetic engineering, and has won numerous awards for her work.

22. "Obesity and its Relation to Mortality and Morbidity Costs," Committee on Life Insurance Research, Society of Actuaries, December 2010, http://www.soa.org/research/research-projects/life-insurance/research-obesity -relation-mortality.aspx.
23. Patrick Canning, Ainsley Charles, Sonya Huang, and Karen R Polenske, "Energy Use in the U.S. Food System," USDA Economic Research Report No. (ERR-94), March 2010, http://www.ers.usda.gov/publications/err -economic-research-report/err94.aspx#.UWcxMhyG2So.
24. For more information on these issues, see also Eric Schlosser, *Fast Food Nation: The Dark Side of the All-American Meal* (Boston: Houghton Mifflin, 2001) and Wendell Berry's books, including his classic *The Unsettling of America: Culture and Agriculture* (rev. ed.; San Francisco: Sierra Club Books, 1996; orig. publ. 1977). See also publications on sustainable agriculture by agricultural extension agents across the country as well as SARE (Sustainable Agriculture Research and Education), which works with the U.S. government to fund grants and provide information for farming projects that promote farm profits, sustainability, and ecological health. Detailed information is also available from grassroots organizations such as the NCAT Sustainable Agriculture Project, headquartered in Butte, Montana; NSAC, the National Sustainable Agriculture Coalition and its many state, local, and university-based participating member organizations; and NFFC, the National Family Farm Coalition, with its own state and local members. See also The Union of Concerned Scientists, "Hidden Costs of Industrial Agriculture" (http://www.ucsusa.org/food_and_agriculture/science_and_impacts/impacts _industrial_agriculture/costs-and-benefits-of.html); "Clean Water and Factory Farms" (http://www.sierraclub.org/factoryfarms/factsheets/ water.asp); Doug Gurian-Sherman, "CAFOs Uncovered: The Untold Costs of Confined Animal Feeding Operations" (Union of Concerned Scientists, April 2008, http://www.ucsusa.org/assets/documents/food_ and_agriculture/cafos-uncovered.pdf).
25. For a discussion of supermarket consolidation and buying practices and the effect on both consumers and farmers, see Elanor Starmer, "Power Buyers, Power Sellers: How Supermarkets Impact Farmers, Workers, and Consumers—And How We Can Build a Fairer Food System," in *Leveling the Field—Issue Brief #3*, http://www.ase.tufts.edu/gdae/Pubs/rp/AAI _Issue_Brief_3.pdf.
26. Dale Allen Pfeiffer, *Eating Fossil Fuels: Oil, Food, and the Coming Crisis in Agriculture* (Gabriola Island, British Columbia: New Society Publishers, 2006), 25.
27. Gary Paul Nabhan, *Coming Home to Eat: The Pleasures and Politics of Local Foods* (New York: Norton, 2002).
28. Barbara Kingsolver, *Animal, Vegetable, Miracle: A Year of Food Life* (New York: HarperCollins, 2007); Alisa Smith and J. B. Mackinnon, *Plenty: Eating Locally on the 100-Mile Diet* (New York: Three Rivers Press, 2007).

29. See for instance Marty Logan, "Agro-Biodiversity in Nepal: Wise Insurance,"IDRCCanada,http://www.idrc.ca/EN/Resources/Publications/ Pages/ArticleDetails.aspx?PublicationID=688.
30. The exact amount of a *cor*, also called a *homer*, is disputed. It is several bushels at least. Later the book of Isaiah will harshly criticize the exploitation of Lebanon's cedars by great regional empires such as Assyria (Isa. 14:8; 37:24). Lebanon's celebrated cedar forests have now mostly disappeared from centuries of over logging.
31. Wendell Berry, "The Agrarian Standard," in *The Essential Agrarian Reader: The Future of Culture, Community, and the Land*, ed. Norman Wirzba (Washington, DC: Shoemaker & Hoard, 2004), 24.
32. Michael Pollan, *Food Rules: An Eater's Manual* (London: Penguin Books, 2009). These are rules #2 and #7.

Chapter 6: The Needs of Animals

1. Many other traditional cultures have used dietary limits and taboos in service of resource conservation; see Firket Berkes, Johan Colding, and Carl Folke, "Rediscovery of Traditional Ecological Knowledge as Adaptive Management," *Ecological Applications* 10/5, 2000, 1251–62, https://www .collaborativeconservation.org/sites/default/files/trad-knwldge-adaptv-mgmt _berkes_etal_2000.pdf.
2. For more on this topic, see Walter Houston, "What Was the Meaning of Classifying Animals as Clean or Unclean?" in *Animals on the Agenda: Questions about Animals for Theology and Ethics*, ed. Andrew Linzey and Dorothy Yanamoto (Urbana, IL: University of Illinois Press, 1998), 18–24. There has been much speculation on the public health dimensions of certain biblical restrictions, such as the forbidding of pork. Houston notes the difficulty of raising pigs in a very dry culture, and the relative absence of pork-eating societies in the surrounding region for centuries before the emergence of ancient Israel.
3. Jacob Milgrom, *Leviticus 1–16* (AB 3A; New York: Doubleday, 1991), 735.
4. This precept is modified in Deuteronomy, which describes only one place in the land—understood as Jerusalem's temple—as acceptable for offering sacrifices (Deut. 12:13–15), and allows for slaughter without sacrifice elsewhere. Even then, the blood, which is considered the animal's life force, is returned to the ground (vv. 16–18).
5. George E. Tinker, "An American Indian Theological Response to Ecojustice," in *Defending Mother Earth: Native American Perspectives on Environmental Justice*, ed. Jace Weaver (Maryknoll, NY: Orbis, 1996), 162.
6. Wendell Berry, *Bringing It to the Table: On Farming and Food* (Berkeley, CA: Counterpoint, 2009), 69.
7. Lynn White, "The Historical Roots of our Ecological Crisis," 5.
8. Charles Birch and Lukas Vischer, *Living with the Animals: The Community of God's Creatures* (Geneva: WCC Publications, 1997), 31–32, citing Jerome's tract against Jovinian.

9. Augustine, *City of God* 1.20, http://www.logoslibrary.org/augustine/city/0120.html. This is not an isolated thought. In a commentary on Genesis he argued that the dominion passage meant: "Let him have power over the fish of the sea and the birds of the air and over the other animals which lack reason, so that we should understand that man is made in the image of God in that respect, in which he surpasses the irrational animals" (*Literal Commentary on Genesis [De Genesi ad litteram]* 3.20 (*CSEL* 28.1:86), quoted in Gillian Clark, "The Fathers and the Animals: The Rule of Reason?" in *Animals on the Agenda*, ed. Andrew Linzey and Dorothy Yamamoto (London: SCM Press, 1998), 71. Her article quotes extensively from several of his writings concerning the inferiority and utility of animals.

10. Thomas Aquinas, *Summa Theologica*, Question 64. Murder, Article 1, http://www.newadvent.org/summa/3064.htm. For more on Aquinas, see Dorothy Yamamoto, "Aquinas and Animals: Patrolling the Boundary?" in *Animals on the Agenda*, 80–89.

11. See Scott Ickert, "Luther and Animals: Subject to Adam's Fall?" in *Animals on the Agenda*, 90–99.

12. Steven Mithen, *After the Ice: A Global Human History* (Cambridge, MA: Harvard University Press, 2003), 34, 77.

13. Tom Leonard, "Cat Predicts 50 Deaths in RI Nursing Home," *Daily Telegraph*, Feb 1, 2010, http://www.telegraph.co.uk/news/newstopics/howaboutthat/7129952/Cat-predicts-50-deaths-in-RI-nursing-home.html; see also the facility's own Web site: http://www.steerehouse.org/shoscar_landing. Geriatric physician David Dosa first discussed the cat in 2007 in the *New England Journal of Medicine*, and has since published the book *Making Rounds with Oscar: The Extraordinary Gift of an Ordinary Cat* (New York: Hyperion, 2010).

14. "Dolphins Rescuing Humans," http://www.dolphins-world.com/Dolphins_Rescuing_Humans.html.

15. See for instance Charles Pinches and Jay B. McDaniel, eds., *Good News for Animals? Christian Approaches to Animal Well-Being* (Maryknoll, NY: Orbis, 1993); Andrew Linzey, *Animal Gospel* (Louisville, KY: Westminster John Knox Press, 1998); Robert N. Wennberg, *God, Humans, and Animals: An Invitation to Enlarge Our Moral Universe* (Grand Rapids: Eerdmans, 2003); and Celia Deane-Drummond and David Clough, eds., *Creaturely Theology: On God, Humans, and Other Animals* (London: SCM Press, 2009).

16. Arsenic has been routinely fed to chickens since the 1950s to promote growth and kill intestinal parasites. In 2011, after an independent FDA study found carcinogenic arsenic in broiler chickens, the drug company producing it, Pfizer, voluntarily suspended its sale (Gardiner Harris and Denise Grady, "Pfizer Suspends Sales of Chicken Drug with Arsenic," *New York Times*, June 8, 2011, http://www.nytimes.com/2011/06/09/business/09arsenic.html?_r=3). The regular use of antibiotics preventively in animal feeds continues to pose human health risks; see for instance Jane

Goodall, *Harvest for Hope: A Guide to Mindful Eating* (New York: Warner Books, 2005), 87–89.

17. Carole Morison with Polly Walker, "Organizing for Justice: DelMarVa Poultry Justice Alliance" (Johns Hopkins Bloomberg School of Public Health, 2007). See also Eric Schlosser, *Fast Food Nation: The Dark Side of the All-American Meal* (Boston: Houghton Mifflin, 2001), 139–42; and Lorraine Mirabella, "Poultry Growers, Chicken Processors at Odds," *Baltimore Sun*, July 19, 2010, http://articles.baltimoresun.com/2010-07 -19/business/bs-bz-poultry-growers-usda-20100712_1_contract-poultry- growers-association-carole-morison-sanderson-farms.

18. United States Environmental Protection Agency, "What is a CAFO?" http://www.epa.gov/region7/water/cafo/index.htm.

19. Environmental Protection Agency, "Regulatory Definitions of Large CAFOs, Medium CAFOs, and Small CAFOs," http://www.epa.gov/npdes/ pubs/sector_table.pdf.

20. Frederick Kirschenmann, "The Current State of Agriculture: Does It Have a Future?" in *The Essential Agrarian Reader: The Future of Culture, Community, and the Land*, ed. Norman Wirzba (Washington, DC: Shoemaker & Hoard, 2003), 105.

21. Bill McKibben, *Deep Economy: The Weath of Communities and the Durable Future* (New York: Times Books, 2007), 55, quoting the *Baltimore Sun*.

22. Michael W. Fox, *Eating with Conscience: The Bioethics of Food* (Troutdale, OR: NewSage Press, 1997), 13.

23. In addition to the discussions by Bauckham, Schlosser, Kirschenmann, McKibben, Fox, and others, cited above, descriptions of factory animal farming may be found in Michael Pollan, *The Omnivore's Dilemma: The Natural History of Four Meals* (New York: Penguin, 2006), 65–84; Ken Midkiff, *The Meat You Eat: How Corporate Farming Has Endangered America's Food Supply* (New York: St. Martin's Press, 2004); Goodall, *Harvest for Hope*, 66–96; Matthew Scully, *Dominion: The Power of Man, the Suffering of Animals, and the Call to Mercy* (New York: St. Martin's Press, 2002), 245–86; Wennberg, *God, Humans, and Animals*, 224–53, and numerous others. In the interest of space, and because the issues are too numerous and detailed to discuss at length here, I merely make reference to some of the most frequently named problems.

24. See the 2001 estimates by the Union of Concerned Scientists in "Hogging It! Estimates of Antimicrobial Abuse in Livestock," http://www.ucsusa .org/food_and_agriculture/our-failing-food-system/industrial-agriculture/ hogging-it-estimates-of.html, and compare with the actual use as reported by the FDA in "2009 Summary Report on Antimicrobials Sold or Distributed for Use in Food-Producing Animals," http://www.fda .gov/downloads/ForIndustry/UserFees/AnimalDrugUserFeeActADUFA /UCM231851.pdf.

25. Alan Durning, "Fat of the Land," *World Watch* 4/3 (May–June 1991).

26. Eric Schlosser, *Fast Food Nation*, 173. He details multiple hazards faced not only by the butchers but, even more, by the sanitation crews who clean between shifts—a job he calls "arguably the worst job in the United States" (177).

27. Farm Sanctuary, "Opinions of Veterinarians and Positions of the AVMA: Analysis of Eight Commonly Occurring Farming Practices, http://www .humanespot.org/content/opinions-veterinarians-and-positions-avma-analysis -eight-commonly-occuring-farming-practices.

28. Barbara Kingsolver, *Animal, Vegetable, Miracle: A Year of Food Life* (New York: HarperCollins, 2007), 228.

29. Jonathan Safran Foer, "The Fruits of Family Trees," *New York Times Magazine*, Oct. 7, 2009, http://www.nytimes.com/2009/10/11/magazine/ 11foer-t.html?pagewanted=all.

30. Derek Thompson, "How America Spends Money: 100 Years in the Life of a Family Budget," *The Atlantic*, April 5, 2012, http://www.theatlantic.com/ business/archive/2012/04/how-america-spends-money-100-years-in-the -life-of-the-family-budget/255475/; "Consumer Expenditures—2011," Bureau of Labor Statistics News Release, September 25, 2012, http://www .bls.gov/news.release/pdf/cesan.pdf; Carrie R. Daniel, Amanda J. Cross, Corinna Koebnick, and Rashmi Sinha, "Trends in Meat Consumption in the USA," *Public Health Nutrition* 14.4 (12 Nov 2010): 575–83.

31. William J. Weida, "Considering the Rationales for Factory Farming," presented at a 2004 Iowa City conference entitled *Environmental Health Impacts of CAFOs: Anticipating Hazards—Searching for Solutions* (http:// www.worc.org/userfiles/file/Weida-economicsofCAFOs.pdf). Weida was an economist in the office of the Secretary of Defense and professor of economics and business in the Air Force Academy and at Colorado College in Colorado Springs, and since retirement has served as director of the GRACE Factory Farm Project and president of the Socially Responsible Agriculture Project (www.sraproject.org).

32. For information on Farm Bill legislation see Institution for Agriculture and Trade Policy, "Farm Bill 2012," http://www.iatp.org/project/farm -bill-2012. For a perspective on the importance of public policy see Michael Pollan, "How Change Is Going to Come in the Food System," *The Nation*, Sept. 11, 2011, http://michaelpollan.com/articles-archive/how-change -is-going-to-come-in-the-food-system/. Also see the Presbyterian Church (U.S.A.), *Food and Faith* blog, http://www.pcusa.org/blogs/foodfaith/.

33. Andrew Grant, "Investigation: Inside Egg 'Factory Farm,'" November 18, 2011, http://abcnews.go.com/2020/video/investigation-inside-egg-factory -farm-animal-rights-group-video-unsanitary-conditions-2020-14987723. See also Steve Karnowski and Derek Kravitz, "Target Follows McDonald's Lead, Drops Egg Supplier Sparboe Farms after Shocking Undercover Video," *Huffington Post*, November 19, 2011, http://www.huffingtonpost .com/2011/11/20/target-mcdonalds-egg-supplier_n_1103770.html, also found

on Fox News, http://www.foxnews.com/us/2011/11/18/mcdonalds-drops
-egg-supplier-over-animal-cruelty-charges/.

34. Susan Mangam, STR, "Sing to the Lord a New Song," *Weavings: A Journal of the Christian Spiritual Life* 7:6 (Nov./Dec. 1992).

35. Scully, *Dominion*, 31–33.

36. "Prayer for the Blessing of Animals," http://members.tripod.com/~Near_to_God/ATprayerfor.html, quoted in Birch and Vischer, *Living with the Animals*, 59.

Chapter 7: Environmental Fairness

1. Steve Lerner, *Sacrifice Zones: The Front Lines of Toxic Chemical Exposure in the United States* (Cambridge, MA: MIT Press, 2010), 84. The term "sacrifice zones" is borrowed from a U.S. governmental term ("national sacrifice zones") for areas dangerously contaminated from the mining and processing of uranium for nuclear weapons.

2. United States Environmental Protection Agency, "Environmental Justice: Basic Information," http://www.epa.gov/environmentaljustice/basics/index.html.

3. Ibid.

4. Kristin Shrader-Frechette, *Taking Action, Saving Lives: Our Duties to Protect Environmental and Public Health* (Oxford: Oxford University Press, 2007).

5. Ibid, 6.

6. Ibid., 17, citing U.S. Department of Health and Human Services and National Cancer Institute (NCI), "Health Status Objectives," *Cancer* 16:1 (1991): 416–40. This figure was confirmed in a 2005 study by the U.S. National Academy of Science: J. Michael McGinnis, "Attributable Risk in Practice," in Institute of Medicine, *Estimating the Contributions of Lifestyle-Related Factors to Preventable Death* (Washington, DC: National Academy Press, 2005), 17–19. Shrader-Frechette cites two other studies by McGinnis and W. H. Foege in the *Journal of the American Medical Association*.

7. Ibid., 18.

8. Shrader-Frechette, *Taking Action*, 16, citing J. C. Lashof et al., Health and Life Sciences Division of the OTA, *Assessment of Technologies for Determining Cancer Risks from the Environment* (Washington, DC: OTA, 1981), 3, 6ff. The disparities between estimates stem at least in part from how health hazards are categorized. For instance, when cancers are attributed to dietary factors, it is often because the foods involved contain chemical pollutants that are stored in fatty foods.

9. Lerner, *Sacrifice Zones*, 9.

10. Ibid., 6. The photo on the book's cover shows a home sandwiched between three smokestacks and four small children.

11. 2011 figure from the National Center for Children in Poverty. Twice that number live below the level for a family of four to cover basic expenses (http://www.nccp.org/topics/childpoverty.html). See David Seith and

Courtney Kalof, "Who Are America's Poor Children? Examining Health Disparities by Race and Ethnicity" (NCCP, 2011: http://www.nccp.org/publications/pdf/text_1032.pdf).

12. Dioxins are highly toxic byproducts of manufacturing plastics, herbicides, pesticides, and paper; of medical and municipal waste incineration; and of coal-fired electrical production. A potent carcinogen, dioxin behaves similarly to DDT and is linked to nervous system disorders, miscarriages, birth defects, immunosuppression, and skin disease. Once it is created, it does not degrade, but remains in the environment and the body for decades.

13. Lerner, *Sacrifice Zones*, 41–69.

14. "Basic Information: What is Superfund?" U.S. EPA (http://www.epa.gov/superfund/about.htm). Love Canal was an abandoned canal in Niagara Falls, New York, that became a dumpsite for hazardous chemicals. When the dump was closed in 1953, Hooker Chemical Company sold the property to the city school district for a dollar. Ignoring leaks, punctures, and exposed chemical drums, the city developed the area for schools and homes. In 1978 a news reporter discovered an abnormal number of birth defects and other ailments among residents. Subsequent studies showed high rates of miscarriage, low birth weight, high white blood cell count, and chromosome damage more than thirty times the expected rate. Eventually the U.S. government relocated more than 800 families.

15. The United Church of Christ report "Toxic Wastes and Race at Twenty: 1987–2007" (http://www.ucc.org/assets/pdfs/toxic20.pdf) pressed for the reinstatement of the Superfund tax, and in 2010 the EPA and Obama administration also pledged support. Since the revenues from heavy industries ran out in 2003, taxpayers have shelled out $1.2 billion per year to pay for the 606 abandoned sites. But more than twice that is needed and the rate of cleanup has dropped from 89 in 1999 to 19 in 2009, according to Juliet Eilperin, "Obama, EPA to Push for Restoration of Superfund Tax on Oil, Chemical Companies," *Washington Post*, June 21, 2010, http://www.washingtonpost.com/wp-dyn/content/article/2010/06/20/AR2010062001789.html.

16. Lerner, *Sacrifice Zones*, 119–36.

17. Shrader-Frechette, *Taking Action*, 22.

18. Wilhelm Harper and W. C. Conway, as quoted in Sandra Steingraber, *Living Downstream: An Ecologist's Personal Investigation of Cancer and the Environment*, 2nd ed. (Cambridge, MA: Da Capo Press, 2010), 48–49.

19. Phil Brown, *Toxic Exposures: Contested Illnesses and the Environmental Health Movement* (New York: Columbia University Press, 2007), 7.

20. David Kreibel et al., "The Precautionary Principle in Environmental Science," http://www.healthytomorrow.org/attachments/kriebel_et_al.pdf, citing C. Raffensperger and J. Tickner, eds., *Protecting Public Health and the Environment: Implementing the Precautionary Principle* (Washington, DC: Island Press, 1999).

21. The capture of scientific research by a variety of means is laid out in Shrader-Frechette, *Taking Action*, 76–112.
22. Ibid., 74.
23. *Living on Earth*, "Earth's Cancer Alley," May 17, 1991, http://stream.loe .org/audio/110408/110408canceralley.mp3.
24. *Living on Earth*, "LOE Retrospective: Cancer Alley," April 8, 2011, http:// www.loe.org/shows/segments.html?programID=11-P13-00014&segment ID=3. Even when industries and politicians resist them, insights like Templet's are reaching the public. According to a recent bipartisan survey by the American Lung Association, 73 percent of voters support stronger pollution controls, believing that we do not have to choose between air quality and economic strength. A two-to-one majority (60 to 31 percent) believe that strengthening safeguards against pollution will create jobs rather than destroy them (http://www.lung.org/about-us/our-impact/top -stories/new-poll-epa-air-pollution.html).
25. Shrader-Frechette, *Taking Action*, 176.
26. Center for Environmental Justice and Children's Help (http://www .nd.edu/~kshrader/cejch.html).
27. The National Religious Partnership for the Environment (http://www .nrpe.org/) makes available denominational statements by the Presbyterian Church (U.S.A.); the United Methodist Church; the Black Churches; and the Evangelical Lutheran Church of America, as well as Jewish, Catholic, evangelical, and ecumenical statements.
28. Lerner, *Sacrifice Zones*, 7–8.
29. This Gallagher plant, operated by Duke Energy, recently closed two of its four units after making illegal modifications that increased its sulfur dioxide output in violation of the Clean Air Act. Sulfur dioxide causes breathing difficulties and, over the long term, pulmonary impairment.
30. For a report on the carcinogenic, allergenic, and hormone disruptive chemicals that are not identified by manufacturers in a number of common household cleaners such as Pine-Sol, Tide, and Bounce, see Women's Voices for the Earth, "Dirty Secrets: What's Hiding in Your Cleaning Products?" November 2011, http://www.womensvoices.org/science/reports/dirty-secrets/. For an extended discussion of the power of transparency to change buying habits, see Daniel Goleman, *Ecological Intelligence: How Knowing the Hidden Impacts of What We Buy Can Change Everything* (New York: Broadway Books, 2009).

Chapter 8: Our Children's Inheritance

1. This is how it is put by such books as Christopher Booker's *The Real Global Warming Disaster* (London: Continuum, 2009). Booker, who, according to the dust jacket, is "the most conspicuous 'global warming sceptic' in the British press," follows 342 pages that intermingle fact and fiction with the equivocal ending, "we cannot yet be absolutely certain of it" (342). A

helpful narrative of the history underlying climate change denying is found in Naomi Oreskes and Eric M. Conway, *Merchants of Doubt: How a Handful of Scientists Obscured the Truth on Issues from Tobacco Smoke to Global Warming* (New York: Bloomsbury, 2010).

2. For example, between 1998 and 2008, ExxonMobil gave at least $23 million to some forty groups seeking to undermine mainstream scientific findings on climate change, including the Marshall Institute, the Heartland Institute, the Heritage Foundation, the Competitive Enterprise Institute, the American Council for Capital Formation, and the Frontiers of Freedom Institute. CEO Rex Tillerson pledged to discontinue this at board members' urging, but it was later found that funding continued. At the same time, Tillerson has begun to argue for a carbon tax that would replace revenue from other sources, such as payroll taxes. See David Adam, "Exxon to Cut Funding to Climate Change Denial Groups," *The Guardian*, May 28, 2008, http://www .guardian.co.uk/environment/2008/may/28/climatechange.fossilfuels; David Adam, "ExxonMobil Continuing to Fund Climate Sceptic Groups, Records Show," *The Guardian*, July 1, 2009, http://www.guardian.co.uk/ environment/2009/jul/01/exxon-mobil-climate-change-sceptics-funding; Chris Mooney, "Some Like It Hot," *Mother Jones* (May/June 2005), http://www.motherjones.com/environment/2005/05/some-it-hot); Eric Pooley, *The Climate War* (New York: Hyperion, 2010), 36, 155; Rex Tillerson, "Promoting Energy Investment and Innovation to Meet U.S. Economic and Environmental Challenges," remarks at the Economic Club of Washington, DC, October 1, 2009, http://www.exxonmobil.com/ Corporate/news_speeches_20091001_rwt.aspx.

3. The story of Duke Energy's CEO Jim Rogers's leadership in negotiating moves to renewable power is narrated in Pooley, *Climate War*.

4. Information here is mostly indebted to David Archer, *Global Warming: Understanding the Forecast* (Malden, MA: Blackwell, 2007); David Archer and Stefan Rahmstorf, *The Climate Crisis: An Introductory Guide to Climate Change* (Cambridge, MA: Cambridge University Press, 2010); and Tim Flannery, *The Weather Makers: How Man Is Changing the Climate and What It Means for Life on Earth* (New York: Grove Press, 2005), with help from other sources.

5. By way of contrast, Mercury, twice as close to the sun, has a very thin, mostly helium, atmosphere lacking CO_2. Despite Mercury's slow rotation and tremendously long days, its daytime temperature is less than Venus's.

6. A metric ton is equal to 1,000 kilograms, or 2,204.6 pounds.

7. Archer, *Global Warming*, 88–89.

8. Flannery, *Weather Makers*, 77.

9. Jessica Ruvinsky, "Fill 'Er Up with Plankton," *ScienceNow* (October, 2003), http://news.sciencemag.org/sciencenow/2003/10/14-02.html.

10. Archer, *Global Warming*, 93.

11. This history is related in Flannery, *Weather Makers*, 38–44.
12. According to Andrew Dessler and Edward A. Parson (*The Science and Politics of Global Climate Change: A Guide to the Debate*, 2nd ed. [Cambridge, MA: Cambridge University Press, 2010], 66), "of the 144 [glaciers] monitored between 1900 and 1980, two advanced and 142 retreated."
13. E. O. Wilson, *The Diversity of Life* (Cambridge, MA: Harvard University Press, 1992), 280. He notes that after each of the five major extinctions, a complete recovery of species diversity required tens of millions of years, a fact that "should give pause to anyone who believes that what *Homo sapiens* destroys, Nature will redeem" (31).
14. "NASA Finds 2011 Ninth-Warmest Year on Record," http://www.nasa .gov/topics/earth/features/2011-temps.html.
15. James Hansen, Makiko Sato, and Reto Ruedy, "Perception of Climate Change," *Proceedings of the National Academy of Science*, Aug. 6, 2012, http:// www.pnas.org/content/early/2012/07/30/1205276109.full.pdf.
16. Archer and Rahmstorf, *Climate Crisis*, 35, 123. For a history of the sunspot claim and the evidence against this, see Oreskes and Conway, *Merchants of Doubt*, 186–90.
17. Archer, *Global Warming*, 116–24.
18. Oreskes and Conway, *Merchants of Doubt*, 173–74.
19. See Dessler and Parson, *Science and Politics*, 61–102.
20. See Ibid., 44–46, for competing theories that were tested before the ozone hole was explained.
21. Ozone (O_2) can be confusing because it raises two different concerns. It is beneficial in the stratosphere, where it filters ultraviolet light, preventing skin cancers. But ozone at ground level comes from sunlight interacting with auto and power plant exhaust, triggering asthma and harming lungs and plants.
22. Intergovernmental Panel on Climate Change, "History," http://www.ipcc .ch/organization/organization_history.shtml#.UCfIjKNmMuc.
23. IPCC *Fifth Assessment Report (AR5) Summary for Policymakers*, 10, 12; http:// www.climatechange2013.org/images/uploads/WGIAR5-SPM_Approved 27Sep2013.pdf. Dessler and Parson (*Science and Politics*, 172) note that "anyone wishing to maintain a supposed scientific basis for rejecting climate action has to attack the integrity of the IPCC," as climate deniers do in various ways. Dessler and Parson carefully show the errors in these arguments (173–74).
24. For the peer review process, see Dessler and Parson, *Science and Politics*, 39–42; and Oreskes and Conway, *Merchants of Doubt*, 269–70. Oreskes, a science historian at the University of California in San Diego, reviewed nearly a thousand scientific papers on climate change published between 1993 and 2003 and was unable to find even one that denied that humans are causing it (Mooney, "Some Like It Hot").
25. For extensive discussion of these claims, see Dessler and Parson, *Science and Politics*, 102–9. For other arguments against action, see 166–79.

26. Archer and Rahmstorf, *Climate Crisis*, 223.

27. Independent Catholic News, "Pope Benedict: Human Development Requires Fighting Climate Change and Poverty," Jan. 11, 2012, http://www.indcatholicnews.com/news.php?viewStory=19632. For full text: http://press.catholica.va/news_services/bulletin/news/28642.php?index=2 8642&lang=it#TRADUZIONE%20IN%20LINGUA%20INGLESE.

28. See Bartholomew's statement at the beginning of this chapter. See also "Encyclical of Ecumenical Patriarch Bartholomew for the Day of the Protection of Natural Environment," Sept. 1, 2006, http://www.oikoumene.org/en/resources/documents/wcc-programmes/justice-diakonia-and-responsibility-for-creation/climate-change-water/encyclical-of-ecumenical-patriarch-bartholomew.html.

29. The 14th Dalai Lama of Tibet, "A Green Environment for Now and the Future," speech made on December 29, 1990, http://dalailama.com/messages/environment/a-green-environment.

30. "Faith and Climate Change," description of a joint religious statement signed at a 2009 meeting hosted by the archbishop. Online: http://www.archbishopofcanterbury.org/articles.php/770/faith-and-climate-change.

31. "The WCC and Climate Change," http://www.oikoumene.org/en/programmes/justice-diakonia-and-responsibility-for-creation/eco-justice/climate-change.html.

32. "Faith and Climate Change," http://nccecojustice.org/climate/.

33. "National Association of Evangelicals Releases Document on Climate Change and Impacts on the Poor," http://blog.nwf.org/2011/12/national-association-of-evangelicals-releases-document-on-climate-change-and-impacts-on-the-poor/.

34. "Climate Change," http://www.presbyterianmission.org/ministries/environment/climate-change/.

35. "A Southern Baptist Declaration on the Environment and Climate Change," http://baptistcreationcare.org/node/1.

36. "Panetta: Environment Emerges as National Security Concern," http://www.defense.gov/news/newsarticle.aspx?id=116192.

37. Elizabeth Montalbano, "Defense Dept. Jumps on Climate Change Research," *Information Week*, November 18, 2011, http://www.informationweek.com/government/security/defense-dept-jumps-on-climate-change-re/231903361. See also the Defense Science Board report, "Trends and Implications of Climate Change for National and International Security" (October 2011), http://www.acq.osd.mil/dsb/reports/ADA552760.pdf.

38. Tim Singh, "Fifteen U.S. Military Leaders Say Climate Change Is 'a Threat to National Security," *Inhabit*, June 1, 2012, http://inhabitat.com/15-us-military-leaders-say-climate-change-is-a-threat-to-national-security/.

39. Damian Carrington, "David Cameron to Make Keynote Environmental Speech," *The Guardian*, April 4, 2012, http://www.guardian.co.uk/environment/2012/apr/04/david-cameron-speech-environment-climate-change.

40. "U.S. Conference of Mayors Climate Protection Agreement," http://www .huffingtonpost.com/2012/08/07/european-commission-climate-change _n_1751031.html#slide=1147365. Though the agreement was to reduce greenhouse gases to 7 percent below their 1990 levels, some cities have achieved reductions as great as 42 percent (L. Hunter Lovins and Boyd Cohen, *Climate Capitalism: Capitalism in the Age of Climate Change* [New York: Hill & Wang, 2011], 16).

41. Ibid., 17. Crist discovered that "implementing aggressive measures to reduce Florida's carbon footprint would *add* $28 billion to the state economy" by 2025. In California, where energy consumption has been held at zero growth since 1974, efficiency has saved the average family $800 per year. "Going forward, fully implementing California's Republican-sponsored cap on greenhouse gas emissions (reducing carbon emissions 80 percent by 2050) would increase the gross state product by $76 billion, increase real household incomes by $48 million, and create as many as 403,000 new efficiency and climate action jobs" (Ibid., 18).

42. EPA Green Power Partnership, "Fortune 500 Partners List," http://www .epa.gov/greenpower/toplists/fortune500.htm.

43. Oreskes and Conway (*Merchants of Doubt*, 242) put the matter bluntly: "Who among us wouldn't prefer a world where acid rain was no big deal, the ozone hole didn't exist, and global warming didn't matter? Such a world would be far more comforting than the one we actually live in. Faced with challenging situations, we welcome reassurance that everything is going to be all right. We may even prefer comforting lies to sobering facts."

44. Lovins and Cohen (*Climate Capitalism*) argue on the basis of hundreds of statistics and anecdotes that whether or not we believe in climate change, the most profitable route for industries, cities, jobs, and national security is to make the changes we would make to mitigate climate change.

45. Ibid., 12–13.

46. Ibid., 137.

47. Ibid., 16–17; Randall Pozdena and Stephen Grover, "Economic Impact Analysis of Energy Trust of Oregon Program Activities," *EcoNorthwest* (April 2002).

48. Daniel Gilbert, "Big Spills from Aging Oil Pipelines," *Wall Street Journal*, April 15, 2013, http://online.wsj.com/article/SB100014241278873237410 04578418693982405224.html?mod=googlenews_wsj.

49. For discussion of the Kyoto Protocol and its outcomes, see Dessler and Parson, *Science and Politics*, 26–29.

50. Worldwatch Institute, "Global Fossil Fuel Consumption Surges," http:// www.worldwatch.org/node/1811.

51. Dessler and Parson, *Science and Politics*, 183. They detail plans for economy-wide, market-based procedures for pricing emissions, creating incentives, supporting renewable energy research and development, and using other regulations and measures as appropriate, with mechanisms to review

and adapt as knowledge advances. Meanwhile, energy corporations are watching for government signals to help them plan future investments.

52. Lawrence Delevingne, "China's Green-Tech Market: $1 Trillion by 2013," *Business Insider,* September 21, 2009, http://articles.businessinsider .com/2009-09-21/green_sheet/30075797_1_renewable-energy-green-building -market-development; Liu Yuanyuan, "China Set to Vigorously Develop Green Economy," *Renewable Energy World,* February 1, 2012, http://www. renewableenergyworld.com/rea/news/article/2012/02/china-set-to -vigorously-develop-green-economy; Lovins and Cohen, *Climate Capitalism,* 23.

53. Jonathan Watts and Ken McFarlane, "China Builds Windfarms in Renewable Energy Boom," *The Guardian,* March 20, 2012, http://www.guardian .co.uk/environment/video/2012/mar/20/china-wind-farms-renewable-energy -video.

54. Thomas Friedman, "The New Sputnik," *New York Times,* September 26, 2009.

55. Ibid.

56. Dessler and Parson, *Science and Politics,* 149.

Chapter 9: Living within Our Means

1. E. O. Wilson, *The Creation: An Appeal to Save Life on Earth* (New York: Norton & Co., 2006), 63.

2. Ibid., 69.

3. A well-designed presentation of the Nineveh palace and the carvings can be found at http://www.odysseyadventures.ca/articles/lachish_slides/lachish _text.htm.

4. James Watt, "Ours Is the Earth," *Saturday Evening Post,* (Jan/Feb 1982), 74–75.

5. Peter Sawtell, "The Shalom Principle," in *Holy Ground: A Gathering of Voices on Caring for Creation,* ed. Lyndsay Moseley (San Francisco: Sierra Club Books, 2008), 208.

6. Ibid, 209.

7. Ibid., 209–10.

For Further Reading

Archer, David. *Global Warming: Understanding the Forecast.* Malden, MA: Blackwell, 2007.

Archer, David, and Stefan Rahmstorf. *The Climate Crisis: An Introductory Guide to Climate Change.* Cambridge, MA: Cambridge University Press, 2010.

Berry, Wendell. *Bringing It to the Table: On Farming and Food.* Berkeley, CA: Counterpoint, 2009.

Bingham, Sally G., ed. *Love God, Heal Earth.* Pittsburgh: St. Lynn's Press, 2009.

Birch, Charles, and Lukas Vischer. *Living with the Animals: The Community of God's Creatures.* Geneva: WCC Publications, 1997.

Brown, William P. *The Seven Pillars of Creation: The Bible, Science, and the Ecology of Wonder.* New York: Oxford University Press, 2010.

Carson, Rachel. *Silent Spring.* Boston: Houghton Mifflin, 1962.

Cohen-Kiener, Andrea. *Claiming Earth as Common Ground: The Ecological Crisis through the Lens of Faith.* Woodstock, VT: Skylight Paths Publishing, 2009.

Davis, Ellen. *Scripture, Culture, and Agriculture: An Agrarian Reading of the Bible.* Cambridge, MA: Cambridge University Press, 2009.

De Graaf, John, David Wann, and Thomas H. Naylor. *Affluenza: The All-Consuming Epidemic.* 2nd ed. San Francisco: Berrett-Koehler Publishers, 2005.

Deane-Drummond, Celia, and David Clough, eds. *Creaturely Theology: On God, Humans, and Other Animals.* London: SCM Press, 2009.

Dessler, Andrew, and Edward A. Parson. *The Science and Politics of Global Climate Change: A Guide to the Debate.* 2nd ed. Cambridge, MA: Cambridge University Press, 2010.

Flannery, Tim. *The Weather Makers: How Man Is Changing the Climate and What It Means for Life on Earth.* New York: Grove Press, 2005.

Goodenough, Ursula. *The Sacred Depths of Nature*. Oxford: Oxford University Press, 2000.

Hessel, Dieter, and Larry Rasmussen. *Earth Habitat: Eco-Injustice and the Church's Response*. Minneapolis: Fortress Press, 2001.

Holmes, Hannah. *Suburban Safari: A Year on the Lawn*. New York: Bloomsbury Publishing, 2005.

Jackson, Wes. *Becoming Native to This Place*. Washington, DC: Counterpoint, 1996.

Kaplan, Jeffrey. "The Gospel of Consumption." *Orion Magazine* (May–June 2008). http://www.orionmagazine.org/index.php/articles/article/2962/.

Kavanaugh, John F. *Following Christ in a Consumer Society*. 25th anniversary ed. Maryknoll, NY: Orbis Books, 2006.

Leonard, Annie. *The Story of Stuff: How Our Obsession with Stuff Is Trashing the Planet, Our Communities, and Our Health—and a Vision for Change*. New York: Free Press, 2010.

Leopold, Aldo. *A Sand County Almanac, with Essays on Conservation from Round River*. New York: Ballantine, 1970.

Lerner, Steve. *Sacrifice Zones: The Front Lines of Toxic Chemical Exposure in the United States*. Cambridge, MA: MIT Press, 2010.

Lovins, L. Hunter, and Boyd Cohen. *Climate Capitalism: Capitalism in the Age of Climate Change*. New York: Hill & Wang, 2011.

McKibben, Bill. *Deep Economy: The Wealth of Communities and the Durable Future*. New York: Times Books, 2007.

Moseley, Lyndsay, ed. *Holy Ground: A Gathering of Voices on Caring for Creation*. San Francisco: Sierra Club Books, 2008.

O'Brien, Stacey. *Wesley the Owl: The Remarkable Love Story of an Owl and His Girl*. New York: Free Press, 2009.

Oreskes, Naomi, and Eric M. Conway. *Merchants of Doubt: How a Handful of Scientists Obscured the Truth on Issues from Tobacco Smoke to Global Warming*. New York: Bloomsbury, 2010.

Page, Ruth. *God and the Web of Creation*. London: SCM Press, 1996.

Pinches, Charles, and Jay B. McDaniel, eds. *Good News for Animals? Christian Approaches to Animal Well-Being*. Maryknoll, NY: Orbis, 1993.

Pollan, Michael. *Food Rules: An Eater's Manual*. London: Penguin Books, 2009.

———. *The Omnivore's Dilemma: A History of Four Meals*. New York: Penguin, 2007.

Schlosser, Eric. *Fast Food Nation: The Dark Side of the All-American Meal*. Boston: Houghton Mifflin, 2001.

Scully, Matthew. *Dominion: The Power of Man, the Suffering of Animals, and the Call to Mercy*. New York: St. Martin's Press, 2002.

Shiva, Vandana. *Stolen Harvest: The Hijacking of the Global Food Supply*. Cambridge, MA: South End Press, 2000.

Shrader-Frechette, Kristin. *Taking Action, Saving Lives: Our Duties to Protect Environmental and Public Health*. Oxford: Oxford University Press, 2007.

Steingraber, Sandra. *Living Downstream: An Ecologist's Personal Investigation of Cancer and the Environment*. 2nd ed. Cambridge, MA: Da Capo Press, 2010.

The Union of Concerned Scientists. *Cooler Smarter: Practical Steps for Low-Carbon Living*. Washington, DC: Island Press, 2012.

Wennberg, Robert N. *God, Humans, and Animals: An Invitation to Enlarge Our Moral Universe*. Grand Rapids: Wm. B. Eerdmans, 2003.

Wilson, E. O. *The Creation: An Appeal to Save Life on Earth*. New York: Norton & Co., 2006.

Wirzba, Norman, ed. *The Essential Agrarian Reader: The Future of Culture, Community, and the Land*. Washington, DC: Shoemaker & Hoard, 2004.

CPSIA information can be obtained
at www.ICGtesting.com
Printed in the USA
FFOW04n0301050417
34202FF

9 780664 233334